# CANADA CUSTOMS

D0746219

# CANADA CUSTOMS

*Droll Recollections, Musings and Quibbles*

To Sandra - all best,

BILL RICHARDSON

Bill

BRIGHOUSE
PRESS
Vancouver
1988

Copyright © 1988 by Bill Richardson

The book may not be reproduced, in whole or in part, in any form (except brief passages in reviews), without written permission from the publisher.
Inquiries should be addressed to
Brighouse Press, #9-784 Thurlow St.,
Vancouver, British Columbia V6E 1V9.

Some of this material has appeared previously in *The Globe and Mail* and on CBC Radio.
The poem in "After the Deluge" is from *The Tassajara Bread Book* by Edward Espe Brown, © 1970 by Chief Priest, Zen Center, San Francisco.
Reprinted by arrangement with Shambhala Publications Inc., 300 Massachusetts Ave., Boston, MA 02115.

Canadian Cataloguing in Publication Data

Richardson, Bill, 1955-
Canada customs

ISBN 0-921304-01-3

1. Canadian wit and humor (English)*
I. Title
PS8585.I34C3 1988 C818'.5402 C88-091444-0
PR9199.3.R53C3 1988

Cover design by Barbara Hodgson
Cover photograph by Jim Labonte
Typeset by Vancouver Desktop Publishing Centre Ltd.
Printed and bound in Canada by Imprimerie Gagné Ltée.

*For my family,*
*both the given and the chosen,*
*with love and thanks.*

"Yes, you may have some of these sweets.
But remember! If you eat too many at once
you will lose your appetite for more."

*Oft-repeated parental warning, circa 1958*

## CONTENTS

## ACKNOWLEDGEMENTS

Some of these pieces have appeared, in somewhat different form, in *The Globe and Mail* and *Q Magazine*. Many have been broadcast on CBC Radio, on "The Afternoon Show" (Vancouver), "Artbeat" (Vancouver), "Arts National", and "The Foodshow."

I would like to thank my colleagues at CBC Radio, most particularly "Afternoon Show" producer Anne Penman, who has been the very soul of indulgence for the last several years; Marg Meikle, bosom buddy, sounding board, and steadfast wailing wall; and the peerless Elizabeth Wilson, whose guidance and friendship have meant more than I can say. And finally, thanks unending to Terri Wershler for her good eye, acumen, faith and bravery; and to David Conlin, who feeds the fish, and with whom I watch "The National."

## CROSSING THE BORDER IN '62

*Lyrics Crying Out For A Country Tune*

When I was a little child
My sweet mama would get riled
By sky-high prices at the A & P just down the block.
"I won't pay that much for bacon!
I'm no fool, I won't be taken.
To raise the cash I'd have to put my family into hock."
In those days of years gone by,
Lordy, Lordy don't time fly,
When it came to pinching pennies my sweet mama was the best.
We'd all hop in Dad's De Soto
Then drive south to North Dakota
And buy up those Fargo bargains till the sun had hit the west.

Oh, give me back those days
Of the North Dakota run.
We were smugglers, we were pirates,
We were bandits without guns.
Lord, we didn't have much money
But we sure had tons o' fun
Hauling Fargo cargo
At the setting of the sun.

Well it might seem quite deranged
In these days of high exchange
To think of bargain hunting down south of the forty-nine,
Though you find it hard to swaller,
Still back then our battered dollar
Hovered close to par with theirs the great bulk of the time.
And the prices were all cheap,
Ma said, "Take a flying leap,"
To hometown merchants who would hike their prices on a bet.
So her parsimonious beacon
Flooded Fargo on the weekends
And we packed the car with all the marked-down goodies we could
get.

Oh, give me back those days
Of the North Dakota run.
We were smugglers, we were pirates,
We were bandits without guns.
Lord, we didn't have much money
But we sure had tons o' fun
Hauling Fargo cargo
At the setting of the sun.

And when we headed on our way
We'd sing along with Doris Day:
We'd all croon "Que sera, sera" while driving through Grand Forks
You know it seemed a fitting tune
For we realized that soon
We'd reach that border crossing with our smuggled beans and pork.
Would they catch us? Would they not?
Would they call our tuna "hot"?
When they asked my Mama, "Ma'am have you got something to
declare?"
Would they bite or call her bluff,
Would they look through all our stuff
And find the soups and stews and jams and Penny's underwear?

Oh, give me back those days
Of the North Dakota run.
We were smugglers, we were pirates,
We were bandits without guns.
Lord, we didn't have much money
But we sure had tons o' fun
Hauling Fargo cargo
At the setting of the sun.

Oh, all the guards there knew our names
And they knew how to play the game,
They all took Mama's word that there was nothing there to find.
When we drove away we'd scoff
'Cause we knew on their day off
They'd be driving south to scoop up bargains Mama'd left behind.
Oh, take me back, Lord, to those days –
At-par dollars and no free trade.
Today there's not one single thing that I would rather do
Than take that cagey hoarder
I called Mama to the border
And bomb on down to Fargo, like we did in '62.

Oh, give me back those days
Of the North Dakota run.
We were smugglers, we were pirates,
We were bandits without guns.
Lord, we didn't have much money
But we sure had tons o' fun
Hauling Fargo cargo
At the setting of the sun.

## SASE

I had a letter from my Uncle Gus in Winnipeg this morning. Shelley, the postwoman, was wearing her stricken look when she came to the door. Shelley has had this route for years and invests her work with a sense of conviction and deep personal interest that is both rare and irritating. She subjects the mail to such close scrutiny, and becomes so attached to her wards that she sometimes finds it hard to relinquish them to the addressee. Shelley forgets that her role is that of stork, not of natural mother. It helps her through the separation anxiety if she names the mail as she hands it over.

"Good news and bad news today," she said when I answered her ring. She was standing in the doorway holding two envelopes, one in each hand. She looked like a travesty of that classic statue of Justice balancing her scales. "There's a letter here from your Uncle Gus."

"Great!" I said. Shelley knows I look forward to hearing from Uncle Gus.

"And then there's this," she continued, holding out a manila envelope on which was written, in my own scrawl, my name and address.

"Oh," I said, my spirits withering, "an SASE."

"Afraid so," said Shelley.

No writer needs to be told about SASEs. They're "self-addressed stamped envelopes." They're part of the etiquette of manuscript submission. You enclose an SASE whenever you send a submission to a magazine or publisher in order that they can more expeditiously send it back to you, in the very likely event they don't want it. Finding an

SASE in the mail can mean only one thing: yet another testament to your personal genius has passed through the bloodstained hands of some pea-brained editor and been found wanting. The SASE is among the most discouraging sights known to man. Even before you open it, you know the verdict.

This SASE was wrapped around my long and innovative poem, "The Cat, the Moon, and the Bloodstone." It was making its way back to home port from the offices of *Canadian Quorum Magazine*. I stared at the envelope for a long time recollecting the sad, rejected and altogether brilliant work that lay within its manila confines.

"Leprous, pock-faced, chill, removed,
The moon sits
At her lunar loom,
Weaving the star-spangled banner
Of treacherous night . . ."

Shelley has brought a lot of SASEs to my door in her time. Since she makes it her business to know everything about her parishioners, she understands that rejection throws a spanner into the works of the rest of my day. She treats each SASE as if it were a black-bordered letter bringing bad news from the front. She worries that one day the camel's back will crack and I'll be driven to some desperate act. Usually she sticks around to offer some solace.

"Aw, what do they know anyway? Some day they'll come banging down your door, and then you can tell them to go to hell. In the meantime, why don't you put on some coffee. That'll perk you up."

"Yes. You're right. Can you stop for a cup?"

"I don't see why not. I'm a quarter of an hour ahead of myself today. Tell you what. I'll get the java together, and you put your feet up and have a boo at that letter from Uncle Gus. That'll make you feel better."

Shelley often finds herself ahead of schedule on those mornings the mail contains a letter with a Winnipeg postmark and Uncle Gus's distinctive scrawl. I always read them aloud for her benefit.

Weeping Willows Home for Golden Agers
December 2, 1986

Hey there, Billy Boy!

We had a bit of an upset yesterday here at Weeping Willows. As you know I'm the editor of our weekly newspaper, The Bark. Every Monday our production committee gets together in the dining room for breakfast and to plan the coming issue. There are usually five or six of us, depending on who's off having a hip replaced or what have you. Well, yesterday Calla May Donnybrook, who's been in charge of our literary page, didn't turn up. Sophie Rice, she's the sports reporter, went up to see if she was all right and found her dead at her desk.

"Calla May is gone," she said when she came back to the table.

"Gone?" asked Vince Jeffrey, the advertising salesman. Vince is thick as two planks nailed together and a terrible gossip besides. The only reason we put up with him is that he's the only one who can work the mimeograph.

"Gone." said Sophie. "Pass the sugar please, Gus."

"Gone where?" shouted Vince, who's getting deafer and louder by the day. "How can she be gone when there's a paper to put out?"

"Vince," I said, "there's no need to shout. I believe that Sophie means that Calla May has passed away."

"Oh dear," said Letitia Winkler. She's our society columnist, features writer, and arts reviewer. "Did you tell someone, Sophie?"

"The girls at the front desk will take care of everything. There's absolutely nothing any of us can do. Pass the cream please, Gus."

"Gone where? Gone where?" Vince shouted. He turned around to the neighbouring table. "Hey! Does anyone know where Calla May's gone?"

At this point, Billy Boy, there was a kind of echo that rippled across the dining room. The words "Calla May's gone, Calla May's gone," were passed from table to table. Before you knew it, the whole place was buzzing.

"Gone? Gone? Did someone say Calla May is gone?"

"Yes. She's gone. That's what I understand."

"For Heaven's sake. What do you think of that? Calla May is gone."

"I saw her yesterday at canasta and she looked just fine."

"Oh no, she looked all grey around the edges if you ask me. I'm not surprised at all."

"Calla May gone? She was always so healthy."

"Went bowling just last week."

"She complained to me about a stomach upset."

"Well, well, well. Calla May is gone."

"Gone where? Will someone please tell me where she's gone?" Vince yelled.

Sophie stood up and leaned into his ear.

"She's DEAD, Vince. D-E-A-D. Dead."

"What? Dead? Everyone! Everyone! Did you know that Calla May is dead?"

Never underestimate the power of a euphemism, Billy Boy. Here at Weeping Willows we can accommodate the word gone easily enough. Dead is a whole lot harder to handle. Within ten seconds, the whole place was wailing.

"Jesus H. Christ," muttered Sophie. She got up from the table.

"Sophie!" said Letitia. "Save that kind of talk for the hockey rink, if you don't mind."

"Come on, Gus. Let's get out of here. I'm right off my feed."

I followed her out of the dining room. We went to the elevator and rode up to the fifth floor where Calla May had lived until her recent going. Neither of us spoke. We seemed to have the same idea in mind. We both wanted to visit her room while it was still quiet. We knew that later in the day there would be a crowd of people coming by to survey the scene of her departure. Also, we were curious to see if she had come up with any copy for this week's paper.

Calla May Donnybrook wrote all her life, right from the time she was a little girl. She'd been writing poetry for us for the last five years, ever since she came to the Willows. Every single issue of The Bark has had at least one of her verses in it. She wrote poems to celebrate anything of note that went on here at the home: people's birthdays, birth of a grandchild, sighting of the first robin in spring, changes in the menu, all that kind of stuff. But she didn't just confine her writing to events of local interest. She scribbled poems to commemorate major holidays and national events, poems about important developments in affairs of state, poems in memoriam for politicians and movie stars when they passed away. Some of them would bring tears to your eyes. You might call this an excess of hometown pride, but we looked on Calla May as the Poet Laureate, not only of Weeping Willows, but of the whole of Canada. No one else could find inspiration in the things that seemed to tickle her fancy. I recall that she wrote a whole series of sestinas about that tainted tuna scandal of a while back. And whenever she wrote something that seemed of national interest, she'd send it off to the big newspapers or the magazines to see if they might publish it. But you know, they never did. They'd just mail her work back to her, in one of those self-addressed, stamped envelopes.

"Wow," said Shelley, "there seems to be a lot of that going around."

I nodded and continued reading.

Why, when the Prime Minister and his wife had their newest baby, little Nicholas, she came up with the most wonderful poem. It went like this.

Oh, let us hone our pencils then
And wield our plumes and Bics,
To cry three cheers for that new child
Who's lately been named Nick.
This scion of the first family
Appeared to loud acclaim,
Too innocent as yet to know
He bears a famous name:
A name that some have heaped with praise
While others have denouced it,
A name that all find troublesome
For how should we pronounce it?
We hear it daily on the news,
And from our friends and cronies,
But no one knows for sure if it's
Mul-Rooney or Mul-Roaney.
This quandary never surfaced with
A Thatcher or a Begin,
(Although it's true that some have wondered
Ree-Gun or Ron Ray-Gun).
And who would fail to heap with praise
The poet who could style a
Device to help us to recall
Your mother Mee-La/My-La.
But we can all be thankful
That of names they could have picked
They chose a simple moniker:
Monosyllabic Nick.
So Tories, Grits, and NDP
As well as fringe persuasions,
Raise your voices and be heard
Now all across the nation:

Hip, Hip, Hooray!

Why anyone with even the slightest grain of editorial sense would decline to print something like that is beyond me. But poor Calla May's work never did appear in any other publication other than The Bark. I figure she was just too far ahead of her time, too much in what you might call the avant garde.

"It's a thankless job for the most part," Calla May would say, "but someone has to do it. I don't really have any choice. That's the way with poets. We're handmaids to the muse. When she knocks, we answer."

As far as Sophie and I could tell, Calla May hadn't managed to compose anything before Death came and scribbled all over her dance card. There were a number of newspaper clippings on her desk though. It looks as though she was preparing to write something about the theft of those microfiche from Revenue Canada, back in Toronto. You know the ones I mean—they had all that personal tax information on them. It has everyone all hot and bothered. I even read that the government is thinking of changing all our social insurance numbers!

"I wonder what Calla May would have found to say about that?" I asked Sophie.

"Beats me," she said, "and it looks as if we'll never know."

I guess not. Calla May Donnybrook is well and truly gone. So anyway Billy Boy, we have an opening here at The Bark for a Poet Laureate. I can't think of anyone in-house who would be inclined to try to fill Calla May's shoes. We don't often print outside contributions, but if you want to submit something I'll certainly consider it. Don't bother sending me that thing about the cat, the moon and the bloodstone though. You read it to me the last time you were in town, and frankly I didn't care for it. Why don't you pick up where Calla May left off? Maybe you can write something about that fellow who nicked all those tax fiche. Maybe you could write something about social insurance numbers. That would be nice. Don't forget to enclose an SASE. Regards to Shelley.

Affectionately,
Uncle Gus.

"I think that would be a wonderful idea!" said Shelley, hoisting her mail bag.

"Social insurance numbers," I said, with a dismissive sneer. "I can't think if anything less worthy of a poem. Methinks *The Bark* will have to look elsewhere for a Poet Laureate."

"Suit yourself," said Shelley, "but it sounds like a great job to me. Catch you on the flip." And she was out the door.

I sat down at my desk, opened the SASE and pulled out my scorned poem. A form rejection letter had been stapled to it.

Dear Contributor,
Thank you for considering Canadian Quorum Magazine. Unfortunately,

your submission does not meet our present needs. We wish we could encourage you to send us more samples of your work; but we have committed ourselves to other writing until early in the next century. Good luck, and again, thank you for thinking of Canadian Quorum.

"Bastards," I said, and not under my breath either. The doorbell rang again. I got up and went to answer it, thinking that Shelley might have left something behind. There, standing on the porch, much to my astonishment, was the Muse. In her hands she held a laurel wreath. She grinned malevolently, and before I could step inside and shut her out she leaned forward and placed it squarely on my head.

"Good luck, sucker," she said. Then she turned, ran down the sidewalk, kicked her heels together and disappeared into thin air.

The next thing I knew I was back at my desk, and my pen was flying across sheet after sheet of paper. Here is what I wrote.

### THE WAGES OF SIN

I beg your kind attention now, the joys of SIN to tell:
No, not the kind of sin that leads the naughty ones to Hell;
I sing the praises of the SIN that's an abbreviation
For Social Insurance Number. These days all across the nation
Our leaders beat their brawny breasts and call out their chagrin
At the sorry fate that has of late befallen SIN.

Oh, who among us ever dreamed our precious privacy
Could fall foul of a fiche-purloining former employee
Of that grand bureau whose good agents doggedly pursue
The false reporters of their wealth and yearly revenue?
But see! The worst has happened and a thief with fingers light
Has made off with those records. His employers, all contrite,
Have cried "Tut tut!" and "Never fear! We promise we'll corral
The cad who cadged the numeros d'assurance sociale."
And though they think the process their computers will encumber
They've said they just might issue us, each one, a brand new number.
This prospect is enough to cow one, hound one, haunt one, daunt one:
A brand new number? Let me say that I, for one, don't want one.

Here are the facts: I have attained the shady side of thirty.
My card is torn and smudged and worn, it's dingy, dark and dirty.
As bank ID a fool could see it would be detrimental:
But none of this can obviate its value sentimental.

I've had the card that I have now for fully half my tenure
Upon this battered planet. When my teeth give way to dentures
I'd hoped that I would have it still, I'd thought that it would last,
A testament, inviolate, to my lost golden past.

I have my card before me now. My adolescent signature
Reminds me of another me: shy, timid, somewhat insecure.
I see myself a callow youth of only sixteen summers
Swelled up with pride upon receipt of that nine digit number
That gave me access to the world of my employment wishes:
Parking cars, and scrubbing johns, and washing countless dishes.
My SIN has come to anchor me in time. When I feel glum
I study it to get in touch with the continuum.
Other numbers in our lives are fickle, transient:
We change our postal codes when we fly after cheaper rent,
Our addresses are subject to all types of transformation,
And phone numbers are party to all manner of mutation.

But SIN remains a constant as we weave our tangled web:
A loyal sheep it blithely goes wherever it is led.
It's always been a given that no loyalty could budge.
SIN sticks by you through thick and thin. It does not carp or judge
Or run away when times get tough, condemn you out of hand.
It follows you no matter where you go throughout the land.
Though years and friends have flown that card stays solid as a rock:
It's always in my wallet nestled 'gainst my right buttock.

As SIN has shown us each such constant love and loyalty
Which one of us would cast if off for petty privacy?
Which one of us would willingly have put before our eyes
Nine new digits it would take a year to memorize?
So join with me! One day you'll see that you a good fight fought!
Damn it! We're Canadians! Let's keep the SINs we've got!

I was flushed and breathless by the time I finished. Hours had passed unnoticed. I placed the poem in a manila envelope, enclosed a covering letter and an SASE. I addressed it to:

The Editor,
The Bark,
Weeping Willows Home for Golden Agers
Winnipeg, Manitoba

Then, arm in arm with the ghost of Calla May Donnybrook, I walked out to the mailbox.

## A RHUME OF ONE'S OWN

At some point in my academic career I took a course in English/French translation. Most of the Gallic morsels we were asked to anglicize were memorably forgettable. One sticks up though, in the saggy mattress of my memory, like a rusty spring onto which I occasionally roll and wince. The troublesome text was a description of the morning after a bacchanalian fete. The narrator, repenting his gluttonous ways, states: "J'ai tellement mangé hier soir que j'ai eu une crise de foie."

The word *foie* was one I was sure I had encountered before in the expression, *ma foi!*, or my faith! I supposed that the *e*, which had been appended to render it foie, was simply there because some sort of gender agreement was required. So convinced was I of my cleverness that I left my Larousse unthumbed and hastily translated the phrase to read: "Last night I had so much to eat that I suffered a crisis of faith."

This did not make a whole pile of sense in the context of the piece, but I reasoned that the French are an angsty bunch who balance precariously on the brink of an existential abyss. It doesn't take much to heave them over, and I supposed that the narrator's overindulgence had provoked in him a realization about the transient nature of the flesh. Imagine my astonishment, to say nothing of my embarassment, when I was held up to my peers as an example of one who had been led away from the straight and narrow path by the infamous *faux amis*, the false friends who hang around in translation's less savoury alleyways. *Crise de foie*, it turns out, has nothing to do with faith and everything to do with digestion. It is literally a liver crisis, a stomach upset, if you will.

I blushed then and I blush now remembering it. I thought it a cruel trick of the French to attach such an abstruse word to such a simple concept. But then I went to France. I lived there for a year, and leaped without looking into the very deepest end of French country cooking. It wasn't long before I earned enough points to win my very own crise de foie. It was quickly apparent to me that the French hadn't been kidding around. The crise de foie was unlike North American indigestion, in both its quality, and in its centre of pain. It was, most certainly, the liver throwing up its hands in despair.

Over the course of that year abroad, I learned that for the French the liver is the seat of the body's government, the throne from which all decrees are issued. Any ailment is blamed on the liver's despotic administration. It has since occurred to me that one of the characteristics that distinguish one nation-state from another is that each population selects an organ or body part to which it can attach some kind of pre-eminence. As the French look to the liver, so the English are all wrapped up in the bowel. Americans are forever going on about the heart and its susceptibility to attack, to arrest, and to breakage. In Canada, we are most preoccupied with the sinus.

I have been unable to trace the socio-cultural reasons for this. It may be because the sinus takes part in that time-honoured Canadian industrial tradition of producing massive amounts of a commodity without reagrd to its usefulness or marketability. It is surely no accident of the language that tons spelled backwards spells what tons spelled backwards spells. Or it may be that there is something to that famous Elizabethan notion of the humours. We are, after all, perceived by the international community as a phlegmatic people.

But let us lay idle speculation to one side and apply ourselves to an examination of some hard facts and to a consideration of their international ramifications. It has been well and frequently documented that women are, either through biology or conditioning, far more able to endure pain than are the males of the species. Here in Canada, as in the rest of the world, the whole weight of responsibility for the public broadcast of discomfort falls squarely on the shoulders of men. At this very moment there are men all across Canada calling attention to their irritated sinuses, in both English and in French. Canadian men, when they have a crise de sinus, are transformed into Lear on the heath, raging against God and nature; or like Goethe, they rise up from a bed of pain and call out *"Mehr Kleenex!"* By elevating sinusitis into a truly Canadian art form we have created, I believe, a rhume of our own. Herein lie the implications for the advancement of the cause of internationalism, particularly with our southern neighbours.

Oh, you men of America! Listen to me! For some years now, our two governments have been blowing on the embers of free trade. You will know nothing of this because your media couldn't give a damn. Ours on the other hand, talk about nothing but the shifting nature of our trade arrangements. It's more tedious than I can say. You need only understand that things are changing between our two countries. It seems that our friendship is going to deepen and expand, whether we want it to or not.

As men and as solid citizens of our two great nations, we have a responsibility to enhance this burgeoning. We must make every possible effort to understand the fuel that powers our separate machines, that is, the American Heart and the Canadian Sinus. If you accept the notion that first impressions are lasting, you will pay close attention to the following brief guide to the art, science, and etiquette of meeting a Canadian man. By bearing these few things in mind, you will be able to apply your own little salve to the cause of international diplomacy when the barriers come down.

When you encounter a Canadian for the first time, bear in mind that he is warier of you than you are of him. His dollar, while more colourful, is generally thought of as being smaller than yours, which causes him a certain amount of embarassment. Furthermore, he has been conditioned from birth by the CBC, by magazines, and by newspaper articles without number to believe that Canada shivers in the cultural shadow cast by your great nation. A certain "my brother, my enemy" principle will come into play in the mind of the Canadian when he first sights you. You can put him at his ease by simply demonstrating that you are aware of the importance of the sinus in his culture. The best way to do this is to affect the following gesture which Canadian men practise.

Place your middle finger and your thumb at the summit of your nose, just south of where it connects to your forehead. Now, rub your index finger all over the sinus area, while making snuffling sounds. This ritual greeting is more or less equivalent to the the muzzle-rubbing indulged in by wolves and other northern creatures to establish trust.

If the Canadian responds in kind, (and if he has any manners whatsoever, he will) he is indicating his willingness to engage in conversation. Try to show him that you have taken the time to learn something about his country. You might drop the names of a few well-known Canadians: Wayne Gretzky, Yvonne De Carlo, Monty Hall, Lorne Greene. Keep punctuating the discussions with allusions to the sinus. Remember too that Canada is a bilingual country. You will warm the cockles of the Canadian sinus if you try a few remarks in French. "Achoo!" is rendered *atchoum!* (pronounced ah-choo!) Offer him a Kleenex, along with a look of solicitude and the simple phrase, *un mouchoir?* (Unn moo-shwar?) Rather more difficult, but well worth the effort is, *ah, mon vieux, que vous êtes enrhumé!* (ah, monn vee-yoo, kuh vooz et on-room-ay). This roughly translates as "hey there, big fella, that's quite a cold you got yourself there."

Canadians love to receive presents and you will advance the cause of friendship considerably if you bring along some American antihistamines, nasal sprays, analgesics, and hot water bottles. When the Canadian sees these, and knows that your intentions are honourable, his nordic reserve will melt away. Before you know it, he will be offering you Canadian quarters so that you can use those shopping mall blood pressure machines. He will be plying you with digitalis. And he will be thumping his left chest and crying out "Angina! Ventricle! Double bypass! Cholesterol!" for all he's worth.

When the ice is broken, you will bask in the hot tub of international understanding. And the next time you meet, on the streets of New York or Dallas, on the boulevards of Vancouver or Montreal, you'll embrace as brothers, heart to heart and sinus to sinus. Vive la différence!

## HUMAN AIRER

Latterly I have been compelled by circumstances well outside the bounds of my control to spend an inordinate amount of time in the air. This flurry of flying marked the end of a long period of blessed abstinence from the dodgy business of battling gravity. Some dozen years ago I was taken over—for no particular reason I can discern—by a kind of intensely rational phobia that made it impossible for me to make the leap of faith required to believe that all those tons of metal could be held aloft by something as remote and difficult to pass in high school as physics. I became possessed by the notion (my therapist called it paranoid, I still think it was sensible) that flyers were the victims of a mass-induced hypnosis perpetrated by the profit-hungry airlines, with the full knowledge and co-operation of the government. As I saw it, this tomfoolery with the public consciousness (accomplished through a complicated administering of mind altering drugs, in tandem with high tech audiovisual aids) tricked gullible travellers into believing they were looking down on the earth from a distance of four miles. It deluded them into stepping from their craft, looking at some familiar landmark (Stanley Park, say, or the CN Tower) and believing it was the Bois de Boulogne, or the Arc de Triomphe.

The only thing I missed about flying, when I finally abandoned it for ground transportation, was the kind of participatory theatre that took place inside an airplane, particularly around the lovely ritual of safety demonstrations. I loved observing all the carefully choreographed gestures that pointed out emergency exits, the delicate ballet that illustrated how to fasten the seatbelt. I watched the donning of the oxygen mask with all the grave attention I would bring to a production of Macbeth, and was always touched to learn yet again that I too had a mask in the little cabinet above my head, poised to jump, at its own peril, to my assistance. I held my breath when they showed off the life preserver, slipping it over their shoulders and taking it to the very brink of inflation. There was always that tingle of suspense: would it, just this once, actually balloon out? But it never did.

It always made me furious to see those few jaded flyers who would pay no mind to this performance. For the most part though, we would all give it our attention and take comfort from it, as children will from a familiar and well-loved story. As I recall, there was a sense of urgency, of necessity, attendant on the safety demonstrations. It was as if we acknowledged the fundamental impossibility of this craft staying aloft, but given that we were all in the same boat, so to speak, we would play along. We all seemed to signal our complicity to believe in this myth for this time, like once a year congregants in a church at Christmas.

The whole mystery of flying was further enhanced by the idea of First Class. I would watch, fascinated, as a couple of the stewardesses—for that is what they were called then—would break off from their sisters like the chosen wives in a harem, and draw the curtains that separated the eunuchs from the sultans. Everyone in Economy shared a prickly sense of voyeuristic curiosity. Who was ensconced in First Class? A President? An Ambassador? Royalty? A movie star? Even before the plane taxied down the runway, you could hear the pop of the champagne corks, hear the bubbly gurgle as the long stemmed Baccarat flutes were filled. You could smell the chateaubriand and imagine the stewardesses donning French maid costumes, fixing their eye makeup, and preparing to minister to the needs of their passengers—all men, all of whom had read *Coffee, Tea or Me?*

Say what you like about class privilege, about egalitarianism. These imaginings, these occasions for the constructions of entertaining fictions, were a comfort to me, stuck as I always was between a colicky baby and a frantic evangelist with halitosis, directly in front of the smoking section which was filled to overflowing with a junior league hockey team, all of whom were learning to drink, and none of whom were quick enough to locate the helpful bags in the seat pockets in front of them.

Now, all has changed. The safety demonstrations are given on video while the flight attendants stand about and plot labour strategies. The excitement, the tension, the edge-of-your-seat feeling that live theatre gives you, is a thing of the past. First Class is now called Executive Class, or Attaché Class. They show it to you as part of the video. Doubtless this is a marketing ploy, a kind of needling to encourage those of us in Economy to work harder, strive higher, pay more! Look! Look! See what you're missing out on!

Frankly, it doesn't look as if we're missing a hell of a lot. First Class – or whatever it's called – is not at all the stately pleasure dome I had imagined. The seats are a little wider, and you can use a telephone if you want. You get a flight attendant with perfect teeth who leans over your seat and says breathily, "Welcome aboard!" There may be a better quality of alcohol available, which is all to the good if you want to pay a whole mess of cash to act like a cheap drunk at thirty-three thousand feet. The meals, as near as I can tell, are the same beige hunks of uncertain origin they serve up to the plebs. And the passengers, it turns out, aren't actors and decadent potentates, but senators, and software salespeople.

So how do you like that? It took me years of therapy to get over my fear of flying, and it's turned out to be yet another disappointment in the shabby charade of life. They've stripped it of its mystery, and now it resembles nothing so much as a form of transportation. So I've given it up again. Now I've enrolled in a course that will take me into a new and exciting mode of travel. It's called "Flying for the New Age." It's cheap. It's safe. And as soon as I find someone who sells astral luggage, I'll be all set to go.

## WHAT THE HAGGIS DID

Claire MacIntosh was loyal
To her family's Celtic roots,
Her lifestyle would be best described as Spartan:
She took cold baths and liked to wear
Severe hairshirt-like suits,
She knew the clans and recognized each tartan.

Her avaricious ways became
A joke among her friends,
Who swore she'd kept the first cent she had earned.
But once a year cheap Claire tossed thrift
And caution to the wind
To celebrate the birth of Robbie Burns.

She would host a party then
Of staggering proportions,
A party that no one could label cheap:
The table was full-laden
And she dished out lavish portions
Of oatmeal cakes and desiccated sheep.

Everyone was called upon
To give a recitation,
The men showed what they wore beneath their kilts.
And when at dawn she sent them home
She'd pack each one a ration
Of haggis, then she'd close the door and wilt.

This went on for years.
Her Burns Day Party was a legend,
The first great fete of everyone's New Year.
For weeks her guests would say
Whenever past good times were mentioned:
"You mean to say you weren't at Claire's? Poor dear!"

But one year it was different.
Claire's mean ways it seemed possessed her
So fully that they would not let her go.
Her party was a misery.
When anyone addressed her,
She'd snap and say, "I don't care! I don't know!"

The food was lean and nasty.
Claire watched with an eagle eye
To see if anyone would go for more.
The guests were so appalled, though,
That they didn't even try;
By midnight she had shown each one the door.

No haggis did they bear away.
They slouched off down the street.
No one called, "Night, night!" or "See you later!"
Claire smirked as she cleaned up the room
And then consigned the treats
To deep within her chill refrigerator.

Tightwad Claire sneered to herself:
"I guess this means I've taken
Care of what to do for next week's meals:
Haggis for my brown bag lunch
And with my morning bacon!
No need to purchase groceries! What a deal!"

She ate her fill all week of that
Scotch seasonal delight,
Her co-workers would watch her and would shudder.
But Claire was undeterred
And she packed for herself each night
An even larger piece of grey, stuffed udder.

But though all week she hacked more off,
And all the next week too,
The haggis no diminishing was showing.
Said Claire, "I may be loco,
But I nonetheless construe
That every time I look, the damn thing's growing!"

Her eyes did not deceive her
For the haggis soon had swollen
Beyond the bounds of her refrigerator.
One night when Claire came home from work
She found that it had fallen
Onto the kitchen floor. "Sooner or later

"This nightmare's got to end!" said Claire.
"These odd hallucinations
Are simply caused by stress or overwork.
I've got to learn to get control
Of my imagination!"
The haggis in the corner pulsed and lurked.

It grew and kept on growing
Till it occupied the kitchen
And then it moved to take the parlour over.
"You're just not there!" said stubborn Claire,
The haggis wouldn't listen.
It slunk and slithered, quivered, hummed and hovered.

The haggis was impervious
To Claire's hard-minded logic.
Each day it just kept growing and expanding.
And then one night it happened that
The comic turned to tragic:
Claire found it waiting for her on the landing.

She had no time to call for help,
To beg or to implore,
No time to ask it why, no time to plead.
It took her 'neath its gruesome arm
And headed for the door.
Poor Claire! She paid a high price for her greed.

Claire has sunk without a trace.
Beware her fate all you
Who have a selfish way of living picked.
The haggis can't be vanquished.
It is waiting there for you,
Somewhere out in the bra bricht moonlicht nicht.

## AFTER THE DELUGE

Some time ago I gave my covivant an aquarium. It was one of those slightly selfish gifts, bought in part to satisfy my own urge to have a pet around the place. Inasmuch as cats make us both sneeze, and dogs need all that walking, and birds are both messy and stupid, fish seemed an ideal choice. Aficionados of things ichthyological assured me that their finny friends had been unfailingly neat, self contained, and easily maintained. So I took the plunge. The gift was well-received, and for most part it was a source of great joy. The aquarium, which we installed in the dining room atop a low bookcase, burbled away, content and blameless. True, one catfish cast an unfortunate pall by going belly-up during a dinner party, and there was a shocking case of mass infanticide among the guppies, but otherwise nothing untoward came our way through the agency of the aquarium.

Then, a few weeks ago, on a Monday, we woke up to find that fully eighteen of the tank's twenty gallons had made an overnight bid for freedom through a tiny leak that had insinuated its way into the caulking. The fish, though distressed, were alive and flipping. They were easily saved. And the hardwood floor had been largely spared because most of the water had been absorbed by the cookbooks that were housed on the shelves beneath the tank. Now that the dust has settled, so to speak, and the fish are newly ensconced in their refurbished home, the cookbooks have emerged as the real tragedy.

It wasn't a huge collection—perhaps fifty books in all. But as I picked through their dripping remains I realized that these were more than mere collections of recipes. Each cookbook symbolized a whole time of life – a time that is gone and will never come again.

Take for example the fishwater-sodden *Kate Aitken's Canadian Cookbook*. I had pirated this classic thirty-five cent paperback out of Winnipeg a few years ago, after a return visit to the parental seat. The book's spine was broken, the pages falling out. Still, it had been a part of my growing up, and it was soggy with sentiment long before it was soggy with water. The cover photograph shows Kate Aitken, that icon of Canadian cookery, draped in the clinical white robes of a professional home economist. She holds a pink-frosted cake and smiles a smile not so much of pride, as of benign encouragement. "Oh, go on," she seems to say, "it's easy! You can do it too!"

Indeed, Kate must have smoothed the way for many culinary novices. I used to read with glee and fascination the cunning "Notes to Brides" that she appended to some of her recipes. These little bon mots were meant to ferry the tremulous new homemaker across the treacherous waters of "Marshlands Chili Sauce," "Golden Fancies," and "Far Hills Apple Dumplings." About "Almond Coffee Ring" she had this to say: "This is a truly delicious roll, one on which you can build a reputation." For my money, this is as telling and as pithy an indicator of the mood and the values of that postwar era as you are likely to find anywhere.

This was the first cookbook I ever used when, as a Cub Scout entirely befuddled by knots and semaphore, I set my sights on the Housekeeper's Badge. In addition to vacuuming a room, and making tea or coffee, candidates for this badge had to prepare a family luncheon. I decided to make French Toast, and turned to Kate Aitken for advice. Following her clear instructions, I made the toast successfully in the traditional way, with eggs and milk. But I promised myself that when I was more accomplished in the kitchen I would scale the heights of epicurean excellence suggested in her "Note to Brides": "For a pungent dish substitute grapefruit juice for milk."

Somehow, though, I was never able to summon up the nerve. When I tossed the dripping Kate Aitken into the garbage bag, I felt a deep sadness at the loss of this token of childhood, this souvenir of a simpler, more innocent time.

*The Tassajara Bread Book* was also drenched beyond redemption. I think it was the first cookbook I ever bought, half a lifetime ago. I was sixteen years old, and was coming to realize that there was a whole other way of thinking and of eating than the one with which I had been raised. This dun-coloured paperback was written by a Zen monk named Edward Espe Brown. It was published in counterculture Berkeley in 1970, and for me it became a symbol of a freewheeling, free-thinking way of life to which I aspired in the full heat of adolescence. The author prefaced the book with a little verse, worthy of Rod McKuen. I committed it to memory. I know it still.

Rock and Water
Wind and Tree
Bread Dough Rising
Vastly all
Are patient with me

*The Tassajara Bread Book*'s stone-ground-whole-wheat-honey-and-molasses philosophy drove a dietetic wedge between me and my family. Following one of the overwhelmingly nutritious recipes, I would make muffins that approximated lumps of granite in their density, and eat them instead of the nasty commercial bread everyone else seemed to prefer. The Tassajara muffins tasted like dust, but I savoured the afterflavour of virtue. Tiny splotches of molasses and honey dotted the pages of that book. They were washed away with the flood, and *The Tassajara Bread Book* was sorrowfully laid to rest in the green plastic garbage bag.

Another paperback, Julia Child's *The French Chef Cookbook*, met a similar fate. I bought this just after moving out on my own. I was dizzy with the sense of newfound independence. Now I was free to apply myself to the unfettered exploration of Fine Cuisine! No more Kraft Dinner for me! I remember feeling that I had attained the very pinnacle of sophistication when I decided to have a celebratory dinner party and serve Julia Child's "Boeuf Bourgignon." I slavishly followed all of Julia's instructions, including the one about peeling and mincing two cloves of garlic. Now, garlic had not been a welcome herb in my parents' home. If some recipe screamed for its inclusion, garlic salt was used instead, and then only sparingly. No one had ever taken the time to teach me that a clove of garlic is one thing, and a head quite another. It took me an hour and a half to peel and mince two heads of garlic. The consequences of this excess can be imagined. Twelve years later it is a dinner party that is still talked about.

One of that evening's guests came by the next day with a housewarming gift, a copy of that universally loved primer *The Joy of Cooking.* "I thought you could use something a little more basic," she said. And she was right. I used it often, and used it well. In fact, I had turned to it the very night of the flood to settle an argument about whether or not turkey should be cooked in foil. (They say no.) It is a hefty volume in the best of circumstances. All sodden, its bulk doubles. It made a sad sound as it landed with its fellows in the bag.

As I tossed out cookbook after cookbook I was struck by what a fickle creature I've been when it comes to food. Half a dozen books reminded me of the year I eschewed all meat. I wished a fond farewell to both volumes of Anna Thomas's *Vegetarian Epicure*, the source of the greatest lasagna recipe ever devised, the lasagna that has become my predictable potluck offering. I bade adios to *Laurel's Kitchen*, a book whose "a woman's place is in the home" preface would have warmed the cockles of Kate Aitken's heart. Goodbye, goodbye I said to *The Moosewood Cookbook*, and to *Recipes for a Small Planet*. It was this latter title, and its companion volume *Diet for a Small Planet* that finally drove me back into the arms of meat when I just couldn't bear the idea of balancing one more incomplete protein.

Disposing of the books that had been gifts was especially poignant. *The Thursday Night Feast,* for instance, was given to me by a friend now dead. The runny inscription and now illegible signature were harsh reminders of how transient a realm is the physical plane. *Beard on Bread* bore the fond wishes of a former love interest. I must confess I took a certain amount of pleasure in chucking it out.

Scattered about in pools on the floor were numerous index cards on which friends and colleagues had thoughtfully transcribed the recipes for dishes at which they excelled. Never organized enough to keep a filing system of these, I had stuck them here and there in the various cookbooks. Now they swore their silent, soggy testimony to my slothful ways.

Recently, I have learned that large academic or public libraries freeze-dry books that have met with watery disasters. This solution never occurred to me. Instead, I took the few titles that looked as if they might be recuperable and put them in a low oven. The pages crinkled as they slowly dried, and the peculiar smell of evaporating fishwater filled the house. It is an odour like no other, and I do not number myself among the blessed for having smelled it. In the end, not a single book was saved.

It was a minor disaster as far as these things go. The fish, at least, came to no harm. And most of the cookbooks can be replaced. I began that task on the afternoon following the flood. I picked up a volume and brought it home. I held it up to the revamped aquarium for the fish to see. It is entitled, simply, *Sushi*. If that damned tank leaks again, we're going to need it.

## CONTINENTAL DINING

I hadn't appreciated the truth of the maxim that travel is broadening until I returned from a recent trip to pastry-laden Europe a full fifteen pounds heavier. Gosh, what a swell old time it was! For five weeks I threw myself at various vendors of sweets and chocolates with an eager promiscuity rarely seen outside those designated areas of Amsterdam. For five weeks my cake-encumbered fingers flew to my lips again and again, with all the surety and delight of swallows returning to Capistrano. For five weeks my right hand feigned ignorance of the delicacies to which the left hand had just helped itself. Thus unrestrained by considerations of conscience, it was able to follow suit. At the end of the five weeks, I was finally compelled to make use of every traveller's trusted companion, the Swiss Army Knife. I did not need it to attack a baguette in the shade of a tree in the Auvergne, or to fend off the advances of a wild boar in the Schwarzwald, or to pry a stone from a horse's hoof in the high passes of the Pyrenees. I needed it in some cafe in Lisbon, to add a little hole to my belt, to bolster its expansive capabilities.

Subsequent contemplation of my ever-widening navel has led me to conclude that the worst part of Going Abroad is the atrocious necessity of taking the body along for the ride. I had certainly not gone to Europe with *gourmandise* at the top of my list of priorities. Oh, no! When I embarked on this excursion my mind was brimming with rich expectations. The mind was out for a full and ennobling experience. The mind wanted to roll around in the featherbed where western civilization was born; to be tantalized by works of genius in galleries and theatres; to be startled by the stony power and arching grace of Gothic cathedrals, to grasp at last which was the transept and which was the nave. The mind wanted to float about on its ethereal own while the body stayed behind in the hotel, neatly folded and stored in the armoire until it was absolutely required. But the body had to tag along, making its incessant, unyielding demands. And my body is a whiner of the first water.

"We hurt," grouse the feet, by mid-morning.

"You're giving us varicose veins," simper the legs.

"Feed me, you fool," growls the stomach.

"I'm going to ache," moans the head.

So it was to placate these lamentably weak vessels that I was obliged to consecrate all that time to sitting about in reataurants and bars and cafés, eating and drinking to excess. All the while the mind was languishing, quietly, unassertively, growing ever more flaccid, like a balloon with a slow leak. Towards the end it gave up altogether and let the body have its untrammeled way.

I realize that this is not the experience of every traveller. Many are more noble. Jesuitical even. They would sneer and point out that the body in question was simply the product of careless breeding and lax discipline. But even they would admit that the rich food, the copious drink, and the high octane coffee that are all impossible to avoid on the Continent lead the body to make demands that not even the strongest mind can quell. And there is one corporeal experience even the most devotedly spiritual tourists must share. Consequently the Toilets of Abroad are certainly the most commonly visited shrines along the pilgrim's path. Oddly, they are among the least described. This has nothing to do with their being unmemorable. Rather, it is because most of us would rather forget them as soon as possible. The eccentric, and frequently unsalubrious state of European public facilities has caused many a North American eyebrow to arch and nostril to flare. On my most recent travels though, I discovered that a new wind has been blowing through the comfort stations of the Old World.

Consider, for example, the concierge. When I first went to Europe years ago the concierge was one of the most astonishing features of continental washrooms. Ostensibly these live-in caretakers were responsible for the well-being and ongoing maintenance of the plumbing. In fact, they were rather more like Cerberus growling at the gates of Hades. Long-toothed guardians of the public good, they took a proprietary view of their establishments. Grudgingly, they would let the public use them. By their gruffness, they reminded their desperate clientele that the baser dictates of biology were not to be sniffed at. To render oneself comfortable was a privilege that was to be taken seriously. It was not with a light heart that one would skip to the loo.

Ah, how well I recall the washroom attendants of Paris! They had attained icon status. I remember them as fierce, withered, antique women, all done up in crisp blue smocks. They were as numerous as gargoyles and at least half as attractive. They put me in mind of garden gnomes who had encountered Pinocchio's Blue Fairy and had achieved something resembling life. They sat in the foyers of those public bogs—which were always subterranean affairs that Orpheus himself wouldn't have strayed near—and knitted perpetual mufflers. They peered at the needy public through a blue haze of Gauloise smoke. They scanned everyone with X-ray eyes, eyes that knew your every need and read your every secret. If asked nicely they would grudgingly hand over a few pieces of waxy, diaphonous paper as you entered. If, on the way out, you failed to leave a *pourboire* of at least fifty centimes in their little basket, they would shriek out Gallic invectives and gypsy curses and barbed-tongued calumnies of a sort that would curdle your blood.

The washroom attendants were among the less sparkling facets of the jewel that is Paris. Nonetheless they were as much a part of the pageant as the third tier of the Eiffel Tower or the mobs around the Mona Lisa, and I was looking forward to renewing an acquaintance with them. *Mais, plus ça change, plus ce n'est plus la même chose.* The washroom dragons are a dying breed. They are being rapidly supplanted by new, high-tech pay toilets that have no need of their fiery services. These unsightly, moulded-plastic, "Johnny-on-the-Spot" edifices have sprung up like champignons all over Paris. I was initially appalled by this burying of yet another tradition. I vowed that I would have no part of it, that I would not be an accessory to this brutal effacing of history. I was determined that I would seek out and use only those lavatories where the human touch, however remote, was still a factor. But, as we have seen, the body will have its way.

On my last day in the city, on the Boulevard St. Michel, Nature spoke so loudly in my ear that in the absence of other options I was compelled to buckle to crass modernity. Against all expectations, it was an event of some poignancy.

These space age toilets cost a franc. You drop the coin in a slot, and the hatch to the cabin whooshes open with an obliging pneumatic sigh. The interior is pleasant, well-lit, and businesslike. A small, reassuring sign above the sink promises that the facility is cleaned and deodorized after each use. Step from the brouhaha of the boulevard into this sparkling, sanitized, chromed Wonderland, and the door eases into place behind you. Whoosh, it says, and invites you to sit. Wondrous things happen. Water gushes from a faucet. Pop music begins to play. American pop music is everywhere in Europe these days—one wonders if there are any indigenous rockers left—and I wasn't surprised to hear guitar-accented English spilling from the speakers that had been incorporated so cunningly into the design scheme. They was something about this song, though, that made me perk up, like a compass twigging to North. This was not American music. It was Canadian. It was none other than Bryan Adams. He was singing "Straight from the Heart." I was amazed. I was moved. It's an engaging song and I found it an appealing sentiment for the occasion—if anatomically inaccurate. Tears welled in my eyes. A wave of nostalgia washed over me. I sang along as best I could, and by the time the song was finished, so was I.

I touched the door, and it breathed a wistful "au revoir" as I stepped back out onto the sidewalks of St. Mich. It thrilled me to think of the chemicals that even then were doing their necessary, efficient job. I was full of a longing for home. I began to hum that little folk song we all learned in the fifth grade, "Un Canadien Errant."

"We hurt!" whined the feet. For once, I wasn't annoyed. I smiled down at them indulgently, and let them take me into a nearby café.

"Oui, monsieur?" sneered the waiter.

"Un Canadian Club, s'il vous plâit," I answered, surprised that he even needed to ask.

## APHRODISIACS

It's coming on Valentines Day, and I'm a mess of hives. Why? Because I'm suffering from gourmet stress. Look, I'm a man of the late 1980s. I've worked hard to become fluent in the languages of food and love. J'adore cous-cous. Ich liebe Haagen-Dasz. This February 14 it had been my intention to bring these two lingos together by making for my significant other and myself a bang-up gourmet dinner featuring aphrodisiac food. But I wanted to be subtle about it. I didn't want to haul out the oysters in a wheelbarrow, if you know what I mean. I wanted to concoct a menu that would propel us irrevoacably and pleasantly towards a natural conclusion, if you catch my drift. I wanted, say, a four course meal that would parallel Ravel's Boléro: a softspoken beginning that gives way to layer after layer of instrumentation, rising to a full and throbbing kind of overblown orchestral crescendo while the camera pans away to Krakatoa exploding, a tsunami destroying Yokohama, the atomic test at the Bikini atoll, and a *son et lumière* show at Versailles, if you follow my reasoning.

With this in mind I went down to the library to do a bit of research. I consulted this book called *The Dictionary of Aphrodisiacs.* It was a major mistake. The author cites the aphrodisiacal wisdom of the ancients, who had some notions that are about as arousing as the idea of a cold shower with Margaret and Denis Thatcher. Here's one of their recipes: "A glassful of very thick honey, 20 almonds, and 100 grains of the pine tree before bedtime. Continue for 3 successive days." Sure thing! And then there was Brillat-Savarin, who suggests grinding up an old rooster (and he does specify "old") with beef, parsley, and turnips. Sounds swell. The author also passes on the aphrodisiac methods of the Amazons, which were not so much dietetic as orthopedic. They used to break the major limbs of their captives in the belief that if the extremities were weakened the naughty bits would be accordingly strengthened. This raises the interesting question of table setting etiquette: do you put the sledge hammer on the right or on the left?

Anyway, by the time I got through *The Dictionary of Aphrodisiacs* I had a shopping list that might have fallen out of the pocket of Ozzy Osbourne. These were items that do not appear in the index of *The Silver Palate Cookbook*. They included dried black ants, dove brains, crocodile teeth, chameleon milk, camel bones, goose tongues, and various other beasty bits that I expect the animals would be loath to lose. I mean, it's all I can do to buy cheese balls, if you see where I'm coming from. And anyway, I figured by the time I made it back from the one deli in Dar es Salaam that actually stocks the stuff, I'd be too tired to keep up my end of the bargain, know what I mean? So sweetheart, forgive me. It looks like it's going to be a box of Laura Secord, a dozen roses, and six oysters on the half shell. What the hell – maybe one of them will have a pearl.

## MODERN LOVE
*Marketing Strategies*

Everyone I know seems to be having trouble on the love front these days. It's not that Cupid has neglected to jab us with his tiny, potent arrows, oh no, far from it. We've all felt their sting, and we've all managed to find ourselves in relationships that are cool, hip, and eighties. In our heads, this is all well and good. The trouble is that our hearts are all gushy, soppy and fifties.

This head/heart conflict is as old as humankind. As the years go by I find it an increasingly difficult one to resolve, especially in February. Lovers the world over are making their fond declarations, buying lacy, heart-laden cards, filled with saccharine sentiments. My heart wants to buy one of those cards. But my head won't let me. None of the verses have anything to do with my situation, nor with the circumstances of anyone I know. The card manufacturers have simply not caught up with the times. Perhaps they think that the extreme convolutions of modern romance are not easily codifiable in the sort of ersatz verse that always lurks inside their products. I am here to show them—and you—that they are wrong. Herewith are four Valentines for right-now people in right-now situations. This is for people who find themselves in commuter relationships:

Though I live in Vancouver dear, and you live in Toronto
I'll still be your Lone Ranger dear, if you will be my Tonto.
And when you move to Ottawa and I am in Ucluelet
I'll still be your Romeo if you will be my Juliet.

I'll leave my heart in Halifax, and you'll leave yours in Chartres,
If you'll be my de Beauvoir, I will be your Jean-Paul Sartre.
And though I go to Winnipeg, and you move to St. John
If you'll be my Madonna, honey, I will be your Sean.
And come the time we've jetted all about this spacious nation
We'll use our frequent flyer points to take a joint vacation.

See how easy it is? And here's a little verse for the people who find themselves breaking up just a few days before February 14:

You took the best years of my life
And ripped them all apart
You passed them through the garburetor
That you call your heart.
You told me lies, you did me wrong,
You broke your every promise,
I took you for a saint
But you were just a doubting Thomas.
You led me down the garden path,
And left me there to pout.
So please accept this candy dear:
I hope that you break out.

Even though sexual mores have changed in the last few years, lots of people still meet through the personals. Here's a Valentine for them:

The moment that I read your ad, I knew you were for me,
And when we met for coffee I was thrilled as I could be,
And when we went for dinner I could only gape and stare
And wonder at the beauty of your lips, your face, your hair.
And after dinner when we sipped our slightly heated brandy
You didn't blanch or quiver when I told you I was Randy.
You said, "I'm randy, too." And now I'm ever so ashamed,
I should have told you that I meant that Randy is my name.

I pray you'll be my Valentine, and hear what I implore:
My name, my love is Randy. Now won't you tell me yours?

And finally, here's a Valentine for those cautious types who want to suggest interest in exploring the possibility of a relationship:

I'm an intelligent adult, and you're equally mature.
Perhaps you'd like to meet sometime so that we might explore
Our two compatabilities. Let's keep it unofficial,
And scan some options that we might find mutually beneficial.
We needn't really go whole-hog into some hot imbroglio,
Or plan to meld immediately our two well-planned portfolios.
I don't suggest that we should jump directly into bed,
Or make an Easter booking at the Guadeloupe Club Med
I only want to tell you with a minimum of dithering,
That you're one of several options I am presently considering.

"The cards I like best," mothers always say, "are the ones you make yourself." Bear that, and these examples in mind, and get down to it. Locating a suitable graphic to accompany your verse is more problematic. I'm going to cut up an old *Life* magazine story on heart transplants. I think that ought to do it nicely.

# REGRETS ONLY

Dear Karl and Rosie:

Thank you for your recent, very kind invitation to your Academy Awards party. You always have such wonderful theme evenings. I'll never forget that fondue fete of a couple of years ago when we were all instructed to come dressed as our favourite cheese. And when I'm feeling down, nothing cheers me up faster than to look at my slides of your more recent "If were a suburb, I would be . . ." effort. I still get all tingly when I remember winning first prize for my representation of Mississauga. Those sprinklers weren't easy to attach, I can tell you! Thinking of these past good times, I am all the more regretful that I must decline to come to the Oscar party. It's simply that I have had nothing to do with the Academy Awards since 1965. Here's why.

In 1965 I was ten years old and had been unhealthily obsessed for some time by Julie Andrews. This unnatural attachment began on the night my parents acquired their first hi-fi set. It was one of those great, hulking walnut cabinet pieces, with built-in speakers and lots of lights. They were endemic to many family rooms in the late fifties. This hi-fi was a castoff from my paternal grandfather, who had moved onto something more state-of-the-art.

Until then our only record playing equipment had been a kiddie gramophone, and the only discs available to us were these thick, brightly coloured vinyl saucers that featured Burl Ives or Gene Autry or Shari Lewis, singing songs like "Big Rock Candy Mountain", and

"Jimmy Cracks Corn." But my grandfather, in addition to passing on the hi-fi, bestowed on us part of his very substantial record collection. They were mostly big band or mood music LPs. They had titles like *Autumn Leaves and Other Favorites.* Their jackets were decorated with pictures of buxom ladies in strapless lamé gowns, smoking cigarettes in long holders while walking little dogs through autumnal woods. (I especially remember one called *In a Romantic Mood* which featured a colour-tinted photograph of a blonde, Monroe-esque woman. She had smiling red gash of a mouth, and her impossibly-angled head was being clutched—forcibly, it seemed—to the chest of a man wearing a corduroy sports jacket. It looked like a photo from a pinup calendar for chiropractors.)

Among these treasures was an original Broadway cast recording of Lerner and Loewe's *My Fair Lady*, with Julie Andrews and Rex Harrison. The jacket illustration was a clever caricature of George Bernard Shaw, represented as God, manipulating a puppet Henry Higgins. Higgins, in turn, was pulling the strings of Eliza Dolittle. On the night the hi-fi came to stay, I was lying in bed in my upstairs room, listening to the strains of Mantovani rise through the floorboards. I was just drifting towards sleep when the music changed. All at once, my ears were ringing to the lyric soprano voice of Julie Andrews singing "Wouldn't It Be Loverly." Karl and Rosie, let me tell you that my reaction was like those people you see on Sunday morning TV who suddenly find their hearts filled with Jesus. What was happening? Had I died and gone to Heaven? This was the most angelic sound I had ever heard! I leapt from my bed and scuttled downstairs, demanding to know who was singing so deliciously. I was told and sent back upstairs where I spent the next forty minutes with my ear pressed to the floor, the better to hear "The Rain in Spain," "I Could Have Danced all Night" and the fiery "Show Me."

A new stage of my development had begun. The very next day, I put away Burl Ives and Gene Autry forever. I claimed that recording of *My Fair Lady* as my very own. I played it over and over again. I drove my parents and brothers to distraction. I learned all the words to all the songs. The day did not go by when I wouldn't sit by the speaker, like a cat before the fire, letting the high, clear, pure voice of Julie Andrews enter my body. I had never heard the word *erotic*, but if anyone had wanted to explain it to me, they would simply have had to say the words *Julie Andrews* and I would have understood. I wanted her as my sister, my mother, my wife. I wrote her long letters, which I never dared to mail. I was a sick, sick lad.

1965 was the year of Mary Poppins. I knew about it well in advance of its arrival in Winnipeg because I had read about it in the movie magazines. (I'd taken to hanging about the drugstore, scouring *Hollywood Mirror* and other scandal sheets, looking feverishly for word of my goddess.) I was thought too young to go to movies on my own, and it was weeks before I was able to convince one of my parents to take me to see it once it came to town. The wait made the experience all the sweeter. Imagine my delight! There she was, filling the screen, dancing, flying through the air, and singing, singing, singing! I was moved beyond words. I wept buckets at the end when she vanished into the skies of Edwardian London, never to return.

Because I kept such close tabs on her comings and goings, it wasn't long before I learned that Julie Andrews had been nominated for something called an Oscar for that performance. I'd never heard of the Academy Awards before that, but I made it my immediate business to find out everything I could about them. It didn't take long for me to figure out that they were an event of some great import. What a feather in Julie's cap it would be if she won. As the day of the Awards ceremony drew near, my excitement quickened. Knowing that my passion had been internationally sanctified, knowing that there were others who felt as strongly about Julie as I did only fueled my fires. I begged to be allowed to stay up to watch the Hollywood ceremonies. I cursed the stupidity of the organizers, who slotted the Best Actress Award at the end of the evening. When finally the moment came, as the names of the nominees were read out, and as the envelope was opened, a terrible tension thudded in my breast. When her name was called, it all burst out of me in a joyous scream. Never had I been happier.

The very next year, Julie was again listed among the nominees, this time for her role as Maria Von Trapp, in *The Sound Of Music*. I'd seen the movie a dozen times by the time of Oscar night. Again, I asked to bend my bedtime rule so that I could watch her triumph once more. The result was a foregone conclusion. There was certainly no contest, for Julie, like the Pope, was infallible. I had not even heard of the other nominees. The presenter opened the envelope, and read out the words, "The winner is Julie"—and again the cheer welled in my throat—"Christie!"

Julie Christie? Julie Christie? Who the bloody hell was Julie Christie? A trollop! An English sexpot who had made some movie called *Darling*, a movie about which no one cared a jot or tittle. What had gone wrong? Who had betrayed my idol? Julie Andrews herself could not have been more upset at the Academy's treachery. At that very moment, I resolved never to watch the ceremonies again. And I never have. And out of stubborn loyalty to that memory, I never will.

What a fickle swain I proved to be in other ways though. Somehow, Julie's public defeat and humiliation crushed my passion. A short time after that I saw Robert Goulet on Ed Sullivan, and a whole new fire was fanned. My life since then, dear Karl and Rosie, you know all about. Enjoy your party and do remember me on Midsummer Night. I'm a terrific Puck.

Your fond,
B.

## WHO IS SHIRLEY?

Of all the environmental perils that we face from day to day, surely none is more frightening or insidious than acid rain. Trees that have spent hundreds of years peacefully numbering their rings and coaxing their taproots deeper slowly melt at its kiss. Anglers pull from once fecund waterways hideous, betumoured fish whose provenance is more fittingly that of nightmare than river or stream. Political leaders wrangle endlessly and to no good effect over how to deal with the situation, and all the while the chimneys of industry belch toxic smoke and fumes skyward. Now, a U.S. team of researchers has said that acid rain damages more than just fresh water systems. It is also contributing to the degradation of Atlantic coastal waters.

I really want to know how Shirley is handling all this. Shirley, you might remember, was the name given to an eleven kilogram male lobster with claws the size of baseball mitts, who was saved by crustacean rights advocates from becoming an Easter dinner in Philadelphia. Shirley, along with an unnamed nine kilogram companion of indeterminate sex, was bought back, packed in ice, and returned to the chill Atlantic off the coast of Maine. It was estimated that Shirley was between forty and one hundred twenty-five years old.

I like to think that even now Shirley is trundling across the ocean floor, snapping his huge castanets, dancing a fandango of joy at having been so unexpectedly reprieved. I wonder if Shirley knows that he was plucked from the frying pan and returned to a slower kind of fire? Will Shirley wake up one morning, say on his one hundred twenty-sixth birthday, and find that his impressive claws have been eaten away? Will he, in all his antique wisdom, see the irony of the situation? Will he let out a little crustacean chuckle of appreciation, then roll over and die?

I went to sleep last night with these cosmic questions in my head. I suppose that's why I was visited in my dreams by no less cosmic a personage than William Shakespeare himself. As we talked about Shirley a sad look came into his insubstantial eye, and he dictated to me this little bit of dreamtime poetry about an acid shower.

Who is Shirley? What is he that everyone defends him?
They saved him from the boorish clods who into meat would rend him,
And reconsigned him to his watery home, full fathom five,
Then crowed, "It's thanks to us that Shirley swam away alive!"

They hied them home and slipped into a deep, untroubled sleep,
And dreamed of Shirley nestled 'gainst the bosom of the deep.
The rain upon their rooftops beat a comforting tattoo,
And Shirley on the ocean floor was glad to hear it too.

He'd heard it for a century, and yet was still enthralled
And pleased to think of how the rain had never failed to fall:
A sound that meant security, a sound to banish fear.
Shirley, dozing, dreamed he'd live another hundred years.

Then let us leave him in his dream and wake up out of ours
And listen to the acid hiss that lingers from that shower.
Let's screw our courage to the post, and write to our MPs!
Let's let King Shirley reign in seas pristine and acid free.

Small, pale tears rolled down his protoplasmic cheeks when he came to the end. I cleared my throat and said as delicately as I could, "Will, you know, this is perhaps not your best work." He said, "When you've been dead 400 years look me up, and we'll see what you can do."

And that's a point well taken.

## SOMETHING TO EXPIATE

Anyone who is deeply committed to the collection of trivia will be aware of the *Harper's* Index, a compendium of unusual statistics that's a regular feature in the monthly *Harper's* magazine. Pick up an issue, flip to the Index, and you've got yourself a ready supply of icebreakers for your next cocktail party. When things get awkward after the introductions, or when conversation flags, you can always perk things up by saying, "By the way, did you know that forty-seven percent of American males would rather have good sex than money, a preference espoused by only twenty-six percent of the women? Did you know that only fifteen percent of conservatives have been skinny dipping, as opposed to twenty-eight percent of liberals?"

One of the Index listings that really caught my attention was the revelation that seven million ant farms have been sold in the past thirty years. This gladdened my heart. While I don't normally approve of zoos or other institutions that keep animals in captivity for the simple purpose of holding them up to human scrutiny, it does seem to me that a special case can be made for safeguarding the lives of ants in a vivarium. Of all God's creatures, ants are among the most vulnerable to attack. This statement, at which some of you will certainly scoff, is born of my personal experience. I have never spoken of it before, but I shall confess it to you now.

Years ago, at the time the first of the seven million ant farms were hitting the market, when I was a tad of a lad, our summertime front lawn in suburban Winnipeg was dotted with anthills. These weren't the enormous, sculpted, tunnel-laced complexes that you see in the pages of *National Geographic.* These were delicate little mounds inhabited by what we called sugar ants. The sugar ants were blameless, innocuous creatures, every bit as sweet as their name. Unlike their larger, warlike cousins, the red ants, sugar ants would wander over a thonged foot and never sink a mandible into a toe. Harmless, friendly, they went about their business assiduously and industriously, wishing no ill on anyone.

My brothers and I were fascinated by these tiny beings, and were curious to learn what their life in the mound was like. Sometimes, in the spirit of scientific enquiry, we would take a teaspoon and dig into a hill. The ants would scurry around in a panic, salvaging eggs and bits of food, bearing them off deeper into the earth. This probing was cruel enough, but it didn't satisfy us. We wanted to see how the ants would react to chemistry. We took a jam jar into the bathroom and made a vile potion of iodine and mouthwash, cough syrup and aftershave, Vitalis and aspirin, Saniflush and Comet. Then we would all pee into it. We shook it up and took it into the yard and poured it onto an anthill. There was no scurry. No rush. Only a silent soggy mound and a noxious odour. We were not content with a single example. We spilled our poison into hill after hill. The results never varied. Finally, when we had enough data, we gave up and went away to pursue other amusements. Probably we pulled the wings off flies.

All children exhibit some degree of sadism. Perhaps we weren't unusual in our refusal to believe that something had a life until we could prove it by taking it away. Luckily, most of us lose this impulse as we grow older. It seems to persist only in certain world leaders.

Confession is a good escape valve for the pressure of guilt, but it isn't always enough to "expiate a pettiness," as D.H. Lawrence put it in his poem "Snake." I'm going to go out now, and I'm going to buy the seven million and first ant farm. And let me tell you, those little guys are going to get nothing but the very best from me, no, nothing but gourmet fare.

## SOMETHING GOING AROUND

*A Desperate Note, Scribbled on the Back of a Soiled Kleenex*

Dear Karl and Rosie:

Please excuse the stationery. It's all these bastards will let me have. How my life has changed since I saw you last week at your very nice "Dress as Your Aspirations" party. (I came as "World Literature," remember?) The very next day I was seized – and am still held captive – by Something Going Around, the insidious organization that is spreading the germ of misery and causing untold suffering across the country. I beg you, Karl and Rosie, get this message to the media so that others may be warned. I can't undertake this myself, as it will be weeks before I can force my way out of this innocuous suburban hideout, where I have been tied to the bed.

It is safe to say that there can scarcely be a Canadian who has not felt the icy touch of this superbly organized terrorist cell. You may know Something Going Around under a somewhat different guise. Its aliases and manifestations are many. It is also known as: "There's a lot of it about"; and "My Aunt Lucille didn't take care of hers, and she almost died"; and "Oh no! Not you too! Everyone at the office has it!"

What exactly is this pervasive meance? Where did it come from? And what can be done to stop it? The questions are all too obvious, but the answers remain veiled in mystery. The most advanced methods and the greatest minds, although they have found a way to put a man on the moon, have yet to find a way of arresting Something

Going Around. It can slip across any border. It can strike at its targets from the air or from a land base. It might be sitting beside you in a restaurant, or breathing down your neck in a bank lineup. Perhaps it is already lurking in your very own home, just waiting for the right moment to pounce.

Once Something Going Around has attained its initial beachhead, it will turn your very bones into its personal piano. It has a large repertoire of misery. Perhaps you will ache, or sweat, or itch. It will put on tiny crampons and scale the slippery slopes of your throat. It will build an encampment behind your eyes and light fire after fire. It will beat on its ritual drums and cause all manner of unpleasant avalanches. It will drive a souped-up Camaro up and down the avenues and boulevards of your body, laying rubber, and hooting its horn loudly at startled passersby.

Something Going Around is impervious to the efforts to expel it as this communiqué, which these hooligans leave lying about the antihistamine sections of drugstores, reveals. I quote it in its entirety.

"You health-obsessed, imperialist cure-mongers! You can do nothing against us! Your Kleenex? Ha! We spit on it! Your Dristan Mist? Stick it up your nose, dog! Your vitamin C? Take as many as you like. We will burn effigies of Linus Pauling in your digestive tract! Your sinus tablets? A joke! Nothing can stop us. Give in to our demands!"

And just what does Something Going Around want? It wants you to ply it with the two opiates without which it cannot be satisfied: chicken soup and aspirin. It will not be assuaged by a hot rum toddy, but will not object to one either. It wants you to lie very, very still and do nothing to disturb it. It wants you to read to it from the collected works of Sidney Sheldon. It wants you to watch "All My Children" and "Three's Company." It wants you to speak only in monosyllables. It wants to be force-fed Belgian chocolates.

Anyone who finds himself in the unshaven embrace of Something Going Around must be alert to the hostage identification syndrome, by which the victim begins to sympathize with the captors, begins to believe in the justness of their cause. For days now I've heard seductive whispers: "Isn't this better than working on that unfinished report? Deadlines, hell! They can wait another week."

But I'm strong. And Karl and Rosie, I can feel my resistance building. These bastards won't be able to break me. One day, Something Going Around will move beyond these borders to find fresh terrain to terrorize. I hope it doesn't come to you. But if it does, give me a call. I know of this deli where they make terrific chicken soup. They deliver.

Yours in congestion,
B.

## HOMEWORK

As a child, I liked the idea of education well enough. But I hated where you had to get it. I was insufferably delicate and priggish about the whole business of school: the jostle, the bustle, the enforced camaraderie, the fusty smell of the lunch room, the sight of other children's sandwiches. I loathed the jangle of the bells and the Pavlovian jolts of fear that ran through me at their bracking. I would do anything to avoid school. I would stay up late reading medical books so that I might convincingly counterfeit the symptoms of new and contagious diseases that would make me a threat to other students. Any ploy of avoidance was worth trying.

The only reprieve from the relentless monotony of it all came on Wednesday. Wednesday was movie day. On Wednesday, we would be shepherded into the gym to watch a scratchy 16 mm film about the life of Pasteur, or the evils of smoking, or the strange ways of foreigners. Once we were shown a documentary about a child's life in the Australian outback. I was unimpressed by the landscape, which was dusty and dreary. I was distressed by the sheep, whose lives of bleating, and chewing, and looking like innocent victims of circumstance were so much like my own. What enchanted me though, was that the child in the film received all her schooling at home, through correspondence and over the radio. Oh, what a lucky hand fate had dealt her! To be able to learn and work at home!

At that very moment I resolved that when I reached an age of self-determination I would work in a domestic environment, surrounded by my familiar creature comforts. I would avoid authority, mindless time-filling, dictatorial timetabling, and any situation that was reminiscent of school. Thus it was, to make a long story short, that I finally became a writer. And I do work at home. I listen for the knocking of the muse, who turns up with ideas other people have already thought of. I listen for the knocking of the letter carrier, who brings me manuscripts editors have not bothered to read. But most of all, I listen to the ukeleles.

You see, I live in a house that abuts directly onto an elementary school. In fine weather my window and the school windows are both open. I am subjected day after day to the rituals of the classroom: the buzzing bells, the scraping chalk, the querulous students and teachers. But all of this annoyance pales next to the ukeleles. What educator ever had the idea that children should learn to strum these genetically deficient guitars? What makes this music teacher think that her students' lives will be enriched by playing over and over again "Silhouettes on the Shade"? How often must they play "La Bamba" until whatever lesson it is meant to convey finally sinks in? How often has the muse given up knocking because I've had my fingers jammed in my ears? How did I screw up my karma? Why is it that I achieved my ambition of working at home, but cannot escape school?

At recess time, I look to the playground below. I feel like Jane Goodall, studying a group of urban apes. There's one little lad who stands apart from the mob. He reads. He listens. Once, I saw him watching me watching. I knew that he was thinking, "Lucky man. He works at home." Child, whoever you are, I can tell that you belong to the fraternity of writers. I know you are dreaming, as I once did, of ways to get out of school. Here's one you might not have considered. Someday soon, go into that music room and smash those damn ukeleles. Claim temporary insanity. You'll get a week's enforced holiday. I'll get some peace. Do it soon, kid. We writers have to stick together.

## METAMORPHOSIS

I bought a leather jacket at the after Christmas sales,
A garment like I'd never owned before.
It cost about as much as posting Claus von Bulow's bail.
I blew the wad and wore it from the store.

I'd never felt so *de rigeur,* so finely fixed and feathered,
So very much in charge, so debonair
As when I donned that pungent swath of black and slinky leather
And stepped into the brisk December air.

I scanned my pale reflection mirrored in the shiny glass
That fronted all the neighbouring boutiques.
I shivered when the other shoppers swiveled as I passed.
I heard them whisper, "Ooh, la la! So chic!"

Now I am not the kind of guy who sets strange hearts to soaring,
I'm not the kind of guy to preen and primp.
I'm dull and ineffectual, conservative and boring:
My mother even thinks that I'm a wimp.

I'm the kind of guy whose name the boss just can't remember,
The kind whose name induces yawns and slumber,
The kind whose phone has failed to ring since sometime last
    September
And then they said, "Oops! Pardon me! Wrong number!"

But when I put the jacket on I felt a transformation,
A sudden shift, a grand apotheosis.
When my detractors saw me in my leather incarnation,
Instead of throwing brickbats, they threw roses.

The clerks gave me the time of day, mechanics didn't snicker
When I steered my failing car up to their pumps.
They just took in my jacket and their interest more than flickered:
It fireballed as to my aid they jumped.

They talked to me in "guy talk," which they'd never done before,
They said "Hey bud," "Hey bro," and "Hey big fella."
I felt as if I stumbled on some secret manly lore,
I felt like Stanley bellowing for Stella.

You'll find it hard to credit that a single pricey garment
Flayed from off the back of some dead cow
Could make a snorting thoroughbred of such a swaybacked varmint:
But I'm the proof, though I can't tell you how.

Since I put the leather on, the phone has not stopped jangling,
More invitations come with each day's post
From some who want to ravish me, and others merely dangling
Bribes and begging, "Let us be your host."

But now the season's changing and with summer fast encroaching
I find that by high noon I'm on the boil.
Unless I take the jacket off I risk demise by poaching
Just like a salmon wrapped in leather foil.

But then where will I be? What else will make crowds hail me?
What else will render me so grand, so cute?
I think I know the answer. So will someone out there mail me
A tightly-fitting leather bathing suit?

## NO RELATION

Surely one of the most telling, yet little celebrated harbingers of the shifting of the seasons is the arrival of the new telephone book. Our revamped White Pages generally migrate to the doorstep at about the time of the summer solstice. This is a sure sign that it is well and truly time to fire up the old barbecue, get the Hawaiian shirts out of mothballs, and check the expiry dates on those daquiri mix kits that have been cluttering the cupboard all winter. Given that the advent of the phone book signals the imminence of such rollicking good times, I always feel a little frisson of delight when I come home and find the new White Pages lying on the stoop like a plump foundling child delivered up by some unseen hand.

However, the joy is short-lived. Self-centred solipsist that I am, the first thing I do when I've manhandled the thing into the house is sit right down and look up my name. Every year this is the occasion for the attack of a two-pronged bout of anxiety. The first comes when I am scanning the impartial alphabetical listings for my moniker. It always takes me a while, since I have been alphabetically challenged from earliest childhood. I begin to panic and sweat. What does it signify if I am not there? Would it simply be an occasion to rant and roar and kick against the telephone company's flaming incompetence? Or should I feel compelled to give way to yet another installment in a continuing series of existential crises? If I am not among the named elect, ought I conclude that I am the object of an invidious conspiracy on the part of all officialdom? If I am not catalogued in the telephone directory, if I am unwillingly unlisted, could this mean that my particulars have been stricken from the records of all bureaucracies? Could I be the victim of a Kafkaesque plot to rob me of my identity, to strip me of all identifying numbers? And if so, does this mean that I am to be cast loose in the world, digitless in Gaza, compelled to undertake some kind of spiritual quest, unknown, unsung, and bereft of all access to government support programmes, including Canada Council Exploration Grants? These may seem like petty and overblown concerns to you, but to me they are very real, and not at all pleasant to contemplate just before dinner.

The second prong of the anxiety attack digs in as soon as I have located my name—which, by the by, I have always managed to do. When I see my name printed in this definitve and very public document, I am seized once again by my sense of what an entirely inadequate name is Bill Richardson. I have never liked it, and I like it less as time goes on. For one thing, it's such a common name. There are always three or four others listed in the directory. And there are hosts of B. Richardsons, who may or may not be Bills, as well as all those W. Richardsons, who are probably Williams known as Bill.

I know that one of the reasons my parents bestowed the name Bill on me was that it is so usual. "We didn't want to give you a name you'd have to fight over," they told me. I appreciate this kindness; but the very normalcy of the name has proven problematic. "Bill Richardson" is all round and soft, like a cream cheese ball at a church supper. It has no hard edges, no unusual or explosive sounds that make it stick in the memory. It is forgettable. I am forever being called Phil Richards or Bob Robertson or Dick Williams. In fact, if anyone shouts out a savoury monosyllable, I answer.

"What's in a name?" asked the Bard in one of his thicker moments. It seems to me that the Kabalarians, those folks who believe that your name really does shape your life, are closer to the mark. In my instance, both my personality and my physical being seem to have taken on the round, soft, inoffensive, and unremarkable qualities of the name.

"Oh spare us your snivelling!" you cry, "If you feel that way about the name, why the hell don't you have it changed instead of whining on about it?"

Would that it were that simple. My years of hoisting around this limp appellation have made me so passive and dull that I don't even have the gumption to start calling myself Buck, or Jock, or Stud, or Butch or Peregrine or Arugula. I can't even imagine making the slight upward jump to the more formal William. Nope, Bill Richardson it is and Bill Richardson it will stay.

Just this morning though, I made a discovery that may spark a much-needed attitudinal change. I was in the library, and I decided that I would look in the card catalogue to see if any Bill Richardsons had ever written a book. I was persuaded that I would find nothing, for who called Bill Richardson could possibly have anything worthwhile to say, and who would be attracted to a book with a cover emblazoned with such an undistinguished handle?

Imagine my surprise when I found that there was indeed a book by a Bill Richardson. And picture my face when I read the neatly-typed title on the catalogue card: *The Ultimate Physique: Bill Richardson's Guide To Bodybuilding.* To say I was flabbergasted would understate the case. I scampered off directly to find this tome and located it alongside muscle guides by men with more memorable names: Schwarzenegger, Atlas. Neither of them though, cuts a more memorable figure than does our Bill. Bill Richardson is a former Mr. World. He is everything that I am not. I am puny and slug-coloured. He is enormous and black. I slouch around as though I carry the weight of the world on my shoulders. He stands tall and proud and looks terrific in a bathing suit. When you look at that Bill Richardson, you think of plumbing. Look at me and you'll think of the kitchen sink.

I sat there with that book for the longest time. I can't tell you what a funny turn it gave me, seeing my name appended to that body. I began to think that perhaps I had spent my life labouring under a misconception. Perhaps the name Bill Richardson needn't necessarily condemn one to a life of servility and stunted accomplishment. Certainly here was an example of someone who had overcome his handicap, flown in the face of the odds, and made something of himself.

"Maybe, just maybe, I could do the same," I thought. I tried to visualize myself as a great, hulking brute. I imagined myself with lumberjack arms, a washboard belly, and pectorals the size of small hills. I stood up, and strode out by the librarians. I'm sure their hearts beat a little quicker in their chests when I passed. I marched by the nasty, officious security guard. "Make my day," I muttered through gritted teeth and stepped out into the street and right into the path of a dressed-for-success executive who was steamrolling past with her attaché case swinging right along the plane of my gonads. Our near collision could have been a whole lot nastier than it was, from my point of view. I spit out my apologies, assuming all blame as is my wont. She didn't take it well.

"Watch where you're going! Are you blind?"

"No," I muttered as she stomped away, "just bland."

As far as new beginnings go, it didn't last long. But now that I've had a taste of life as a he-man, life as that Bill Richardson must lead it every day, I at least can sense that change is possible. I'm going to work on it. And when the next phone book is delivered, I'm going to flip to my name right away. I'll look at it hard. And if I don't like what I see, I'm going to rip that goddam phone book in two and swallow it whole.

## LOVE HANDLES

I've just peeled off my bathing suit, the one I bought last summer,
A skimpy Speedo outfit, cherry red, a real stunner.
So scant it was that when I wore it out to catch some rays
I hardly had a tan line at the closing of the day.

Last summer I was fit and thinner than a fasting monk
But since then I've expanded in the region of my trunk.
And just now when I donned the suit and strutted all exuberant
Before the glass my sides were flanked by fleshy flabs protuberant.

"My God," I muttered bleakly as I stood there, "What a scandal!
I've reached the stage of middle age! Behold, my new love handles.
Oh how can I go out again, and lie upon the beaches
Encumbered as I am by these appalling, fatty leeches?"

I jumped up once or twice and then suppressed a silly giggle
On noting as I landed that they flapped a bit, then jiggled.
"Whatever have I done," I asked, "to merit these two shoddy
Tenants in the temple that I used to call my body?

"Could it have been that lemon pie? How many pints of beer
Have trickled down my gullet since about this time last year?
It might been a side of fries that I declined to share,
Or possibly that chocolate cake – I gobbled every layer.

"Of course, there was the piggish night when I refused to stifle
My lusting after more dessert, and trifled with a trifle.
And at a potluck just last month, I set my jaw and mustered
The gall to maul a tray of tarts, then blustered through the custard.

"And though they call them handles, one would scarcely want to pick up
Such an unattractive package." I suppressed a tiny hiccup,
And giggled once again as my two fenders flopped anew.
A sudden inspiration dawned! I knew what I would do!

I'd buckle down, apply myself, just like a hardened stoic
To regimens of sit-ups, push-ups, pull-ups and aerobics.
I'd see myself as Sly Stallone, and cling to his example,
And drive these chubby infidels from out the body's temple!

To celebrate the day when from their clutches I'd be free
I sat right down and gobbled up a half-thawed Sarah Lee.
I chased it with a quarter pound of sticky peanut brittle,
And then, exhausted, laid me down, to slumber for a little.

I dreamed a dream wherein I was a hale and hearty eighty
My friends had kicked at seventy, content and rich and weighty.
And I was left alone as one by one they up and died,
Not even these two wads of flesh left clinging to my sides.

When I awoke my mind was clear, I'd come back to my senses.
I saw my handles as my friends, and not as rude offenses.
If someone wants a bathing suit, I've one I won't be needing;
I bought myself a muumuu, and I'll spend my summer reading.

## ONE MAN'S METER

I am not a Luddite. Indeed, some of my best friends are machines. I have no objection whatsoever to people who are smarter than I am inventing devices that are smarter than I am to make my life easier. However, there is one recent technological advance that causes me grave concern. Someone, doubtless annoyed at being caught yet again at a parking meter with insufficient change, has started marketing a computerized meter that operates with a credit card. You use the card to check in and out of your parking spot, and at the end of the month you are billed by the municipality.

"Well, grand!" I hear you say. "No more having to load up with quarters and dimes every time I head downtown." But allow me to warn you against the late twentieth century misapprehension that convenience is everything. I have been dealing with parking meters for sixteen years now and have grown very fond of them. I like them just as they are and do not want to see them altered in any way. Here are some of my reasons.

To begin with, I am terribly afraid that the reformers might decide to change the clunky shape of the meters. This would be a catastrophe! Who, on a bright day when the sun is shining just right, has not been delighted by how closely the shadows cast by double headed meters resemble Mickey Mouse ears? How often have I been shaken from my habitual glumness by this happy coincidence? How often have such felicitous sightings swept aside dark musings on old personal slights in favour of jolly recollections of Annette Funicello?

If the shape of parking meters is tampered with, one of the great chances for unsolicited public happiness will be lost forever.

And if the need for depositing change into parking meters is eliminated, what will become of that lovely slogan "Police Will Not Turn Handle"? Everytime I read that silly caveat my mind races with ever more ludicrous imaginings. Police will not turn handle! Well, who would ever have thought that they might? Do police officers have to take some kind of vow before they receive their badge, a vow that they will never "turn handle"? How must this affect their lives? Do they spend hours waiting for people to open doors for them? At Christmastime, do they get to hear only one side of the *Messiah*? After all, police will not turn Handel. Are their domestic lives constantly disrupted by disputes over unpleasantness in the bathroom? How often is this little scene acted out?

"For Heaven's sake, Marv! You're 34 years old! When will you learn to flush?"

"How many times do I have to tell you Sandra? Police will not turn handle."

By reading those five simple words in the right way I can practically snicker myself apoplectic. Psychologists say that laughter is good for you. Losing "Police will not turn handle" would be detrimental to my mental health. Do the meter changers want to take responsibility when I go off the deep end?

And let's not discount the effect that changing the meters will have on the state of romance in this country. The journals of Cupid are overflowing with the names of people who have fallen in love with shopkeepers; with affairs, marriages even, that began with someone simply going into a store to beg some change for the meter. From there, it's just a hop, skip and a jump to chats about the weather, the stock market, and what are you doing for dinner?

If none of this has convinced you, then perhaps I can reach you through appealing to base self-interest. Just last week a friend of mine tried to force a coin into the mouth of a meter. It wouldn't swallow, so she gave it a sound slap. Its little door fell open to reveal its guts. Immediately she understood why it hadn't co-operated. It was already full! Being a good-hearted soul she naturally wanted to make the meter comfortable, so she scooped out most of the nasty excess. Voilà! It felt much better! And it worked just fine! Now just think about it. As things stand, every meter-bearing street is a potential Las

Vegas. Would that be the case if these credit cards take hold? No. It would not.

From all I've told you, it should be plain that I feel quite passionately about preserving the traditional parking meter. But I acknowledge that there must be those out there who feel equally strongly about implementing the credit card system. Doesn't it just go to show that one man's meter is another man's poison?

## THE PROPHECIES OF AUNT EUSTACIA

I had a letter from my Uncle Gus in Winnipeg this morning. Shelley the postwoman stopped for a quick coffee, the way she sometimes does, especially on mornings when the mail includes something with a Winnipeg postmark and Uncle Gus's distinctive scrawl. I read it out loud for her benefit.

Weeping Willows Home for Golden Agers
Winnipeg, Manitoba
May 2, 1988

Hey there, Billy Boy,

I've been a tad worried about you out there on the west coast, what with all this stuff that's been in the paper about this Nostradamus fellow.

"Nostra-who?" I asked Shelley.

She gave me her what-planet-do-you-live-on-anyway look.

"Nostradamus. You know, the famous 15th century French seer. He's reputed to have predicted everything from the Industrial Revolution to the rise of Hitler to the time the Queen Mother nearly choked on a fishbone. His prophecies came to him as little poems. There's been a lot about Nostradamus in the news these days because he predicted that the whole west coast would crumble into the ocean, sometime in May. Orson Welles made a film about it years ago. Apparently all kinds of Hollywood hotshots have taken it quite seriously, and they've gone to visit relatives in Tulsa for a while. I read that Joan Collins went back to London until the coast is clear. You really should make more of an effort to stay on top of the news." Shelley has a way of putting you in your place. I continued with the letter.

> Now you know that I don't put a whole lot of faith in this psychic stuff, and normally I wouldn't be concerned at all, except for something I recollected about your Aunt Eustacia. You might not remember her. You weren't more than a wee mite when she passed on. But she had herself quite a reputation out there around Starbuck as a fortune teller.

"Starbuck?" asked Shelley.

"Starbuck, Manitoba," I said with appropriate scorn at her ignorance and continued reading.

> Eustacia would always have a little booth at the church bazaar and the Strawberry Tea, and she'd read tea leaves and such. There were people who swore she told them things only they could have known. She was forever warning folks in Starbuck that they were about to die or get married. She told me about your Aunt Adele even before I'd met her. And if Wes Reimer had only listened to her, he'd be alive today. Well, maybe not. He'd be about 106. But at least his tractor wouldn't have rolled over on him. Sometimes Eustacia would go off into a kind of trance, and she'd write these prophecies. She always wrote them in poems, just like that Nostradamus fellow, and when I started reading about him in the paper I recollected that Eustacia had had a few things to say about earthquakes too. I dug around through some old trunks, and I came up with her diary. I'm sending you the appropriate pages, because I thought you might be interested.

I looked at the enclosed diary excerpts. There were four poems, written in a fine spindly hand in lavender ink. They were prefaced with this cryptic remark, "These signs forebode a shaking of the westlands." Shelley took a swig of coffee and leaned forward expectantly in her chair. I read the first one out loud. It seemed to presage the pasta revolution.

From Caesar's soil shall sprout a food
The new world will call tony,
A thousand variations on
That staple, macaroni:
Tortellini, Fettucine,

Orzo, Rigatoni!
Ravioli, Penne, Gnocchi,
Kreplach, Tortiglioni!

Fresh pasta any time of day
Shall be their fondest credo,
All served up with spaghetti sauce,
Or with a fine alfredo.
And this shall be the sign that spells
The endtime for all sinners:
When children scorn Chef Boy-ar-Dee,
And no one buys Kraft Dinner.

I felt a chill rush up my spine, and Shelley let out a low whistle. "That's astonishing," she said. "Come to think of it, I don't know a soul who buys Chef Boy-ar-Dee anymore. And my sister's kids turn up their noses at Kraft Dinner."

I nodded. And there was more. Aunt Eustacia would never have heard of IKEA, or of unassembled furniture, or of any of the Scandinavian trends in home furnishings. And yet, she seemed to foresee its ascendancy. She wrote:

The hardy, northern Viking race
Shall rally and supply
A trendy line of furniture
That everyone will buy.
I see the tall white bookcase,
I see the couch of chintz,
I see the glass-topped table
Where you eat your Sunday blintz.
I see the nifty standard lamps,
The chairs and dishes too.
I see you crushed beneath them
When they fall on top of you.

Shelley and I exchanged frightened looks and cast our eyes nervously at the looming bookcases on either side of the room.

"Go on," she said, "read the rest."

I did. How on earth could Aunt Eustacia, who lived all her life in Starbuck, have divined the White House astrology scandal as revealed in *For the Record*, the book by former Chief of Staff Don Regan? More than thirty years ago, she had written:

The day will surely come to pass
As sure as Rome was pagan,
When someone's who's called Regan
Spills the beans on one named Reagan.
This Regan will say Reagan was
Possessed of senses fleeting:
And most inclined to stay supine,
And fall asleep at meetings,
Then hem and haw and fly off
On extraordinary fancies,
And follow the directions
Of his spousal unit, Nancy.
This Nancy steers her crazy course
By frequent consultations
With sages who interpreted
The shifting constellations.
When all is told their spacious ranch
Will shudder, heave, and break up.
It's doubtful though that Reagan
Will be troubled or will wake up.

"Oh my gosh!" exclaimed Shelley. "This is giving me the creeps. Look, here's the rest of your mail, I have to run."

She handed me a few bills, and my copy of *People Magazine*. The cover photograph was a wedding picture of longtime Hollywood sweethearts Burt Reynolds and Loni Anderson.

"Wait!" I said. "There's just one more. Don't you want to hear it?"

"Oh. All right. How much worse can it get?"

She had her answer as soon as I read Aunt Eustacia's last prophecy.

When hunky Burt and lovely Loni
Finally tie the knot,
And gladly trundle off to find
Their warm connubial cot,
You can be sure these prophecies
Will finally be proved:
When Burt and Loni hit the sack,
The earth is sure to move.

Shelley let out a shriek and headed for the door. I've never seen a woman with a full mailbag run so fast. I finished reading Uncle Gus's letter.

> It's your birthday coming up soon, and I haven't seen you in a long while, so I'm enclosing a plane ticket to Winnipeg. You can use it any time, but just in case it might influence your decision, that Nostradamus fellow pegged the big earthquake to happen on May 9. Regards to Shelley.
>
> Affectionately,
> Uncle Gus.

May 9? A niggling something crept up behind me. I went to the calendar to see if my suspicions were correct. They were. Today is May 10. If there had been an earthquake, I'd missed it. I checked the postmark on the envelope. It was stamped May 2. It had taken over a week to get from there to here. It was a good thing Shelley had taken off with such celerity. I might well have been tempted to use her as a scapegoat for the inadequcies of the system. I took her mug to the sink and muttered an assortment of unpleasant things while I washed away her lipstick stain: peach, which is new for her. And then I sat down with my calendar and planned my visit to Uncle Gus.

## POSTCARDS

Great travellers have always been meticulous keepers of journals. They fill notebook after notebook with their impressions of over the hills and far away. Then they publish their memoirs so that armchair travellers can vicariously hear the sound of the camel bells, whiff a spice market, or see (and smell) one of those massive Tibetan statues carved of yak butter.

Unfortunately, I have just never had the discipline required to sit down at the end of a day of fevered sightseeing and keep a diary. But the fact that one is lazy doesn't mean that one can't be ambitious, and I still hope to join some day the ranks of Marco Polo, Mary Kingsley, and Paul Theroux. My medium of recollection, however, is not the journal. It is the postcard. I write them by the score in those empty moments that come up in the middle of the travelling day—waiting for a museum to open, a train to come, or a cappuccino to cool. I welcome the challenge of packing as much information and style into those tiny confines as possible. Once it is done, I send the gem-like aphorism to one of a select group of trustworthy friends, to someone I know will preserve the thing in a camphor chest, pending the day I become famous and even my old grocery lists will be in demand and eminently collectible.

The obvious fly in my ointment is that it relies on the co-operation of the post office—not just here, but abroad. However, in all the years of my perigrinations my method has never failed me. Not a single postcard has ever gone astray.

Now, I recently returned from three weeks in China. I confess that I had a few qualms when I first started to record the discharge of my overloaded senses and give them up to the tender mercies of the Chinese mail system. What were the chances of a meek postcard's survival in whatever mechanism has been devised to distribute the mail to a billion people? Would the inside workers understand English script? Happily, my doubts were quickly put to rest by an article in the English language paper *The China Daily*. It was about a postman named Wang Jinsheng. Wang is thirty-one. He carries an average of seventy-six kilograms of mail on his bicycle and rides eleven kilometers to 540 households, twice a day. He is renowned for his skill at reviving dead letters. Since 1980, the paper said, Wang has rescued no fewer that 718 letters that had been given up for lost; 173 were from outside the country.

"Whenever I see these dead letters," he is quoted as saying, "I feel they are like eyes, yearning for help."

Such dedication, to say nothing of such poetry, made me feel positively cheerful about the fate of my precious cargo. And so, full of confidence and more stimulated than I had ever been by the shocking newness of everything, I redoubled my efforts. I sent off card after card, into the box's black void and out over the South China Sea. For three weeks, I inundated my friends with my precious and unique insights into a strange land.

It is true that the foreign media do not sit up and beg for scraps of news from the table of Canadian current affairs. It was not until I came home that I learned this country had been embroiled in yet another round of postal strife. Imagine my sense of betrayal! I had been so concerned about the reliability of foreigners that it had never occurred to me that a spanner might be tossed into the works in my own home and native land.

What is wrong with our postal workers anyway? What has happened to their sense of priority? Don't they understand that they have jeopardized an important future document? Don't they see that the creation of a national literature is more pressing than petty considerations of job security?

To date, about seventy percent of my cards have arrived. Where are the others? At the bottom of some mail bag? Trampled on the sorting room floor? Have they joined the ghostly ranks of great lost manuscripts? Will the truth ever be known?

In the midst of this bleak, black bereavement there is but one ray of consolation. Perhaps, years hence, a friend will hear a knock on the door and open it to find a shy and exhausted Chinese postman on the stoop. It will be Wang Jinsheng, a world removed from his appointed rounds, come from afar, through the sleet and snow, to deliver up the postcards we had taken for dead.

## 'GATOR GUS

I had a letter from my Uncle Gus in Winnipeg the other day. It arrived on the morning after we'd had one of those untoward incidents that make one seriously question the wisdom of being a householder. An enthusiastic rain had been falling steadily for the better part of a week. Its relentless exuberance was getting to us all, and tempers were becoming noticeably frayed. Minor crackups and collapses can be expected at these times. But who would have thought the basement sewer would have been the first to break down?

"I can't stand it anymore!" it must have shrieked. "Have you any idea what I have to deal with?" And it proceeded to show us, spilling all the secret resentments it had harboured, lo these many years.

I was in my gumboots, dealing with the sludgy remnants of its catharsis when the doorbell gave its tintinnabular summons. I am not the sort of person who can ignore bells. If I am in the shower and the phone rings, I charge out all naked and vulnerable and sopping to answer it. If I happen to hear to the pealing of church chimes, all manner of pious and utterly bogus longings come to the fore. And if the doorbell sounds, even if I am in the midst of the most intimate recreations, I am compelled to see who requires something of me. Why is this, I wonder? Perhaps I was one of Pavlov's dogs in a previous life. In any case, looking like a mud wrestler, cursing whatever ungentlemanly caller was waiting without, and hoping against hope that it wasn't the Witnesses again, I slopped up the stairs and across the kitchen linoleum, leaving an unfortunate trail in my wake.

I peered through the window and saw Shelley the postwoman standing on the porch, water pouring off her peaked cap and down her slicker. I opened the door.

"Whew," she said, wrinkling her nose at the musty waftings that had followed me from the basement. "What's up? Have you been making cabbage rolls again?"

I was not of a mind to put up with this kind of derision and fixed her with a killing stare.

"I see," she said. "Well, I can tell you're busy, and I won't take up any more of your time, even though I am about fifteen minutes ahead of schedule. Even though I can see a full pot of coffee on the stove. Even though a cup of java would certainly hit the spot right now. You don't need to drop a ton of bricks. I can tell that's out of the question. So I'll just deliver this letter from your Uncle Gus and continue on my appointed rounds. In the rain. In the wet. In the cold."

"Oh shut up," I said, and stood back so she could come in. We sat at the kitchen table, poured a couple of cups, and read the latest news from Uncle Gus. Prescient as ever, he had written about sewers.

> You must have been reading, Billy Boy, about how the mayors of this great country's fair cities are all up in arms about their sewer systems. Seems that they've been there too long without any improvements–the sewers that is. Some of the mayors, too, come to think of it. Now they're saying that all kinds of terrible things are going to happen unless they fix those sewers up, and pretty darn soon, too.

"Maybe they're right," said Shelley, looking at my gumboots. I read on.

> These mayors are all saying that they should get help from the provinces, and the provinces are saying that they need help from Ottawa, and Ottawa is saying that sewage isn't a federal responsibility, and if that isn't a setup for a cheap joke I don't know what is. Now, if they're going to go down there and start fixing things up, all I really want to know is who I have to call to find out what they're planning to do with the alligators.

"Oh come on," guffawed Shelley. "No one believes those stories about pet baby alligators getting flushed into the sewers and turning into Godzillas!"

> Oh, you might scoff, but it's true. They're down there and they've been

around for quite some time now. I know because I've seen them myself. Wrestled one of them in fact, and that's a yarn to tell. It happened over fifty years ago. I'd been courting your Aunt Adele for a good many months, and I finally summoned up the nerve to pop the question. In those days a fellow was expected to provide an engagement ring and to bring it with him when he asked a girl if she wanted to get married. The ring was a considerable financial outlay, and it was a sign that he wasn't a mere trifler.

Picture this, then. Here I was all suited up in my finest duds, wearing a new tie, and with my shoes so polished I could see the reflections of the stars in them when I looked down. I'd stopped at the jeweller's on the way over to see Adele, and I was carrying this little box—the one with the ring inside—in one hand, and a bouquet of flowers in the other. I was strutting along peacock proud, admiring my reflection in a store window, not watching where I was going, and I didn't see this slab of loose pavement. I tripped over it and that ring box went flying off into the air and fell down the sewer.

I can hardly tell you how distressed I was! Mad too. That ring wasn't cheap, and I couldn't feature myself turning up to ask a girl to marry me and telling her, 'Oh, by the way, I lost the ring down the sewer.' The more I thought about this the madder I got. That old adrenalin started pumping, and before I knew what I'd done I'd pried the cover off the nearest manhole, and climbed on down. Whew! It was rank. I won't trouble you with the gory details, Billy Boy. I'll leave it to your imagination. Suffice it to say that you wouldn't want to open up a Club Med in such a place. There was a narrow little walkway to stand on. I lit a match and peered around and sure enough, there in the middle of the canal was the box floating just as nicely as a velvet boat, and its precious cargo still intact. I figured that if I reached out with that bouquet of flowers I could just reach it. I was just about to do that, when this huge alligator loomed up out of the murky depths and swallowed that ring box.

"Holy smokes," said Shelley, "that's incredible! Where'd it come from?"

Probably you're wondering how it got there, and in retrospect, so do I. But right then and there was hardly the time or the place for reflection. All I knew was that an alligator had swallowed my ring and I wanted it back. I didn't even think what I was doing. I just shook that bouquet of flowers at him and said "Gimme back that ring, you sewage-swilling son of a gun!"

All I can figure out is that he must have been allergic to those roses, because he opened his mouth wider and wider, and started making these noises that sounded for all the world like someone getting ready to sneeze. Quick as a wink, I took off one of my shoes, and jammed it between those two rows of jagged, nasty teeth to keep his jaw open. Then I stuck my hand right down his gullet and pulled out the box. Just in time, I might add, because when that sneeze let fly, those jaws snapped shut with a noise like a vault door slamming, and my shoe was gone for good. If looks could kill I wouldn't be here today. That 'gator fixed me with such a stare! It makes me break out in a sweat even now to think of it.

Half an hour later, there I was at your Aunt Adele's door carrying that little ring box and some wilted looking roses. Her mother wouldn't let me in. "Gus is outside," I heard her say, "he's wearing one shoe, and his suit is ripped, and he smells like he's been wrestling alligators in the sewer. He says he has something to ask you."

Adele never was troubled by undue curiosity. She figured that what people did was their own business, which I think was to her credit. She invited me to sit down on the porch swing and didn't ask me anything except would I like some lemonade? And when I popped the question she didn't even look surprised, and she didn't mind having to wipe off the ring with her hanky before she put it on and the rest, I guess, is history.

I figure that pretty soon they're going to go down there and start cleaning up those sewers, and I think that they might be surprised at some of the things they find. And Billy Boy, that's why I want to find out who I contact to apply for one of those alligators. I figure I'm owed a pair of shoes. Regards to Shelley.

Affectionately,
Uncle Gus.

"Too much," said Shelley, shaking her head as she got up to go.

She opened the fridge on the way out of the kitchen, and scooped up a bagel. "Thanks for the coffee," she said, and I followed her to the door. The downpour had stopped, and a rainbow arched its way over the hardware store across the street.

"Shades of Noah," she said, and went on her way, leaving me to my gumboots, and the basement.

# LOONETTE

It was a hot day in June when I met September. I'd had one of those uspeakable, tension-riddled times at work, one of those days when one begins to take the whole notion of karma seriously. Whatever offences I might have committed in some previous life, I was now being repaid in spades. You've been through the same mill at one time or another. I won't trouble you with the details.

Standing up on the bus going home, I tried to put the stress of the last eight hours behind me by practising that new age trick of visualization. I called to my mind, like a great vision out of *spiritus mundi*, a picture of a glistening gin and tonic. I fixed it firmly in my head. I could taste the distillation of juniper on my tongue, could smell its happy bitterness. It was an olfactory prophecy of what I would concoct for myself once I got home. Gin! It would be my solace and my reward.

I put the bus behind me, and let the fantasy sink down tap roots. I watched that glass of G & T grow and grow until it had acquired the dimensions of an Olympic-sized swimming pool. I was its sole inhabitant, shooting up and down its lanes, propelled by strokes brawnier than anything I might achieve in real life.

I was so taken up with these imaginings that I went right by my stop and indeed was almost a mile beyond my accustomed point of descent when I finally came to. I jerked the bell and stepped from the bus into the hot blast of the day. Reality leapt over some neatly-trimmed suburban hedges and slugged me in the gut.

"You fool!" hissed Reality. "How will you realize your fantasy? Have you forgotten Noreen?"

I had. Noreen, my martini-loving cousin from Saskatoon, had blown into town the week before for the Amway convention. For three days she had stayed with me, drinking my Beefeater and singing raucous hymns in praise of a whole roster of soap products. Now there wasn't a drop of gin in the house.

My fantasy melted before me like some towering six dollar ice cream cone that had come to grief on the scorching pavement. Disconsolate, I turned and aimed myself homeward. That was when I saw September. She was reading, seated at a little table beneath an improvised canopy that she had festooned with streamers and crowned with helium-filled balloons. There was a large banner strung across the canopy, emblazoned with the gaily painted words: SEPTEMBER'S KOOL-AID.

*Kool-Aid*! It had been years since I had thought about Kool-Aid. A kind of *nostalgie de la goo* came over me. If I could not take comfort in the tangy privileges of adulthood, I would banish the tarnished present with a brief paddle in the sticky waters of childhood. I crossed the street.

The child looked up from her book, and regarded me with the kind of serious demeanour cultivated by clerks in stores like Saks Fifth Avenue. She appeared to be nine or ten years old. She was wearing a baseball cap on which her name, September, had been appliquéd. Her T-shirt, which read "My grandpa and grandma went to Las Vegas and all they brought me back was this lousy T-shirt," hung halfway down her jeans. She wore the grimy hightop sneakers so prized by youngsters of her generation.

"How much for the Kool-Aid?" I asked, in the saccharine voice used to address children by those of us who are barren-loined and entirely witless about just how savvy youngsters – especially nine or ten year old girls – have become.

"Seventy-five cents."

"Seventy-five cents?" I parroted incredulously. Even accounting for inflation this seemed a disproportionate increase from the going rate of that long ago summer when I too had opened a Kool-Aid stand. It was, mind you, a very different kind of operation.

I had set myself up on a card table that had gone wonky when a member of my mother's bridge club had reacted violently to her partner's moronic bid. The table's consequent starboard list had rendered it useless for gaming, inasmuch as ashtrays and bowls of chips might at any moment precipitate themselves floorward. Outdoors it was not such a threat; and the sugar-loving ants were grateful for the occasional pitcher of Kool-Aid that toppled onto the grass.

I worked out of our backyard, which was well out of view of the street. In this way I didn't attract a lot of customers, and wasn't compelled to worry overly about the ugly necessities of commerce such as marketing and making change. I installed myself under the cascading boughs of a weeping birch because it was cozy and because it was that much farther out of the public eye. Such was my stealth that anyone might have thought I was operating a still. I charged a penny a cup and, as there was but one vessel to be had, only one person could drink at a time. The only flavour I carried was Cherry. This was because other varieties—Grape, most particularly—stained the tongue, and were sure giveaways to parents that their children had been drinking in the middle of the afternoon rather than saving their allowances for their college educations. There were no regular hours for this little Kool-Aid can, and word of its availability on any given day was spread wholly by word of mouth. I was only interested in servicing a select clientele of friends, all neighbours. In fact when intruders from one street over actually got wind of the enterprise and appeared at the gate with their pennies in hand, I flatly refused them service. You could never be too careful.

As the summer went on some of my customers—envious of my success and covetous of the pennies that seemed to be in vast supply in those days—set up their own stands. The fickle public, always hungry for something new, gradually stopped coming by. Slowly my business trickled away. I didn't much mind. I would still make Kool-Aid when the spirit moved me, sit under the weeping birch, and slug it back myself if no customers turned up. I enjoyed it. To this day, I find no stigma attached to drinking alone.

"Seventy-five cents firm," said September. "I don't dicker. And it's a dollar for our diet line. *You* might be interested in that."

She looked significantly at my midriff. A few years ago, had I been a robber given to knocking over convenience stores, a sharp-eyed clerk would have described me to the police as having "thinning hair and a slight paunch." Now, "verging on bald and with a pronounced spare tire" would be closer to the mark.

"Diet line?" I asked, speculatively. "As I remember this stuff is half sugar, half water. How can you have a diet line?"

"We use Sweet 'n' Low. That's the reason for the mark-up."

"I see. Well, seventy-five cents for a glass of Kool-Aid still seems a tad steep to me."

September rolled her eyes skyward, put down her book—a copy of Lee Iacocca's autobiography—and looked me straight in the eye.

"Look, I'm aiming at an upscale market. I deliver a quality product. I offer four flavours in both the diet and the regular line. My overhead is considerable. Look at these streamers, and balloons. You think these cost nothing? I use high quality disposable plastic glasses: none of your dixie cups stolen from the community centre washroom for September's Kool-Aid. And I stand behind every unit I sell. I make it in the blender, so that the customer won't be troubled by graininess, and every glass is icy cold. If you want quality, you've got to pay for it. So it's seventy-five cents."

I reached into my pocket and extracted three quarters.

"I'll take a regular Cherry, please."

"Regular?"

"Please."

She gave me a "the customer is always right and anyway it's your funeral" kind of look, and poured it out. I drained it in a gulp.

In a Proustian instant, I was back in Winnipeg, under the lovely green branches of the weeping birch. All of childhood passed before my eyes, rickety and crazy and scratchy like a cheap 8 mm cartoon. This was plainly a reaction September had seen before in her adult customers. She indulged my reverie for a few seconds before clearing her throat and saying, "It's fifty cents for a refill." I held out the glass and a dollar bill.

"September is a nice name," I said as she made my change. "Is that the month you were born?"

She sighed the sigh of the stricken. "No, thank God. That's a great way for naming puppies and islands, but not children. I was born in April. My mother called me September because she thought it captured a mood, or something. You know: happy and sad at the same time. The smell of burning leaves. I suppose it could have been worse. She might have called me 'Christmas Morning.' Or maybe 'The Roaring Twenties.' As soon as I turn eighteen I'm going to have it changed."

"To what?"

"Maybe Joanne. I kind of like Joanne. When you're called September everyone expects you to wear flowers in your hair and sing like Judy Collins. Besides, when we get to California, I bet that every second girl is going to be called September. Or Autumn. Yuck! Joanne will be more unusual."

"You're moving to California?"

"Next month. My mother is going to find her clown."

"She lost her clown?"

"No, she hasn't found it yet. Care for another?"

I handed over another couple of quarters. Something in my look must have broadcast my bewilderment.

"See, my mother has been in the clown business for a few years now. She calls herself Loonette. Maybe you've seen her posters." Loonette did sound familiar to me, although for a moment I thought it was just because I had once lost my glasses in Montreal. Then I remembered the posters I'd noticed on neighbourhood lamp standards and construction walls. There was a cartoon clown captured in mid-pratfall, and the slogan "Let Loonette Liven Your Life! Parties! Barbecues! Office Functions!"

"She does all that usual clown stuff. She goes to mall openings and birthday parties. She ties balloon animals and squirts people with a seltzer bottle. She's good at it. Everyone laughs. But she says that even though she gives the appearance of knowing what she's doing, inside, something's missing. She says she still has to find her clown."

"But what does that mean?" I asked, feeling more stupid by the second.

"Beats me. It was the same way when she went to est a few years ago, and found IT. She talked about it for weeks afterward. 'What's IT?' I kept asking. And she'd say, 'It's IT. You know when it hits you.' Finding your clown is the same kind of thing. It means that you go around looking ridiculous, and humiliating yourself in front of crowds. But you really understand why you do it. Apart from the money of course."

"I see," I said, although I didn't really. "And why will she find this clown in California?"

"Oh, there's a Clown School there. It's run by some guy called Loony Toony who was a big noise in the sixties. My mother figures that if anyone can help her find her clown, he can. She's really looking forward to it. She figures it'll make us a stronger family unit as well. She says that we'll be much closer than we are now because finding her clown will help her get in touch with the child inside her."

We fell silent for a moment. I sipped my drink and looked beyond the Kool-Aid emporium to the unassuming bungalow behind. The Kool-Aid seemed to have awakened the X-ray vision I was able to summon up when I was a child. In those days, I was severely addicted to the adventures of Superman. So were my brothers and the other boys in our neighbourhood. They would wrap towels about their necks to serve as capes, and jump from the tool shed roof in a pretense of flying and preternatural strength. I had no time for these limb-threatening recreations. My only interest was in peering through erected barriers, and seeing hidden things. I looked right through the stucco of the bungalow, and saw very plainly how all the remnants of September's mother's discarded enthusiasms lay scattered about inside: the herbal teas, the essential oils, the Yoga manuals, the esoteric texts on Tibetan Buddhism, the tatty paperbacks that explained to women why men hated them, the half-baked pottery projects. I looked into September, looking to see if some trace of a child remained. I thought I saw one, huddled and shivering in a corner of her heart.

September looked at her watch and squinted up at the westward-leaning sun. She began to roll up the awning.

"What about you," I asked, "do you want to go, too?"

"Oh sure. There's lots of opportunity down there for expansion. With the money I make here I'm going to buy a juicer. They're much more health-conscious in California, and this sugary stuff just won't sell. Besides, we'll be near the Valley."

"San Fernando?"

"Silicon. I'm quite interested in computer applications for my business. One for the road?"

"Sure," I said, and reached for some more quarters.

"Nope. This one's on the house. Buy three, get one free. That's my deal."

"That's a good marketing tool. You didn't mention that before."

"I just made it up now. Flexibility. It's the key to survival."

She cut the strings on the balloons and their dwindling helium spirits took them heavenward.

"Cheers. And good luck," I said, draining the Kool-Aid in a gulp.

I walked home through the late June afternoon, the days already on the downward slide into winter. I wondered if September had ever read Superman, or Supergirl. You can argue that it's commercial schlock, but I think it's a useful myth to grow up with. It feeds the fantasy of being from another planet, of having come into one's parents' lives entirely by accident rather than design. There are moments in growing up when that's a good idea to have as a point of reference.

I had the better part of a mile to walk home, and by the time I got there the four glasses of Kool-Aid were hammering at my bladder. Nevertheless, before I turned the key, I stared hard at the door, willing its atoms to give way. But wood and brass were all I saw. I couldn't catch even a glimpse of what lay on the other side.

## PERPETUAL ADOLESCENCE

**A** few years ago, I began noticing a change in the dental geography of my friends who were teetering on the brink of their thirties. Many of their mouths—which had once been distinguished only as the destination of forkfuls of pasta and as the source of endless bon mots—were now sparkling with scaffolding. What I mean to say is, they were suddenly wearing braces. I wanted to know why. Was it for cosmetic purposes? Were they tired of beaver jokes, tired of being called Buck? Had they always borne a grudge against the quirky jutting of a particular incisor? Or were they doing it for medical reasons, to correct an over- or under- or side-bite of some kind?

Oddly enough, none of them seemed very sure why they had invested so much money and so much future discomfort in this hardware. When quizzed they would simply shrug and say, "Oh you know. It seemed like a good idea. I never had them when I was a teenager."

This statement reveals two things. It reveals that the trend in adult orthodontics is yet another symptom of my generation's unquenchable thirst for status. Braces are a kind of BMW of the mouth. People wear them, in part at least, as jewelry, as a visible sign of economic arrival. They wear them, more than any other reason, because they can afford them. If they haven't got money to burn, they at least have money to burnish.

This trend also reveals a generational reluctance to relinquish the things of youth. Braces, ever since their invention, have belonged to teenagers. How many of us in our thirties can recall any of our parents' generation wearing them? They invested their money in items more appropriate to adulthood—televisions and dishwashers and second cars. These were the thoroughly grownup things they bought as signs of maturity. But then, as they never tired of reminding us, they had lived through the Depression and the Second World War. Tough times compelled them to grow up fast. If you didn't get braces when you were a kid—too bad! But our even greater prosperity has allowed us to chase after that most elusive commodity—youth—by clinging to its outward signs. Like braces.

And acne. Which of our parents complained of acne? They, very sensibly, just stopped having it after the age of eighteen or so. They got on with their maturity. Occasionally something they called a blemish might have erupted on a forehead or cheek, but it didn't cause trauma or a marriage breakup. Now, every time you pick up a lifestyle magazine you find some article on the horror of adult acne. Cosmetic counters are buckling under the weight of the creams and potions one can purchase to deal with the blight. The only reason our common concern with acne has remained undiminished over time is that we haven't had to grow up. We have remained happy-go-lucky teenagers, buying expensive versions of souped up jalopies, partying to excess, staying thin, worrying about zits, straightening our teeth, and listening to rock music. The great floating bubble of our infinitely expanding adolescence has made us a prosperous, confident, and flaky lot.

And now we have arrived at the dangerous end-years of the century. The dire words of the millenarians clutter the press. Scientists warn of the dangers of global warming and the greenhouse effect. The earth gasps for breath through the pollutants we spill into it, and all the while the economy teeters on the brink of computerized collapse. Perhaps the bubble of our extended adolescence is about to burst. Pehaps we are about to witness the greatest collective maturation the world has ever seen. It's been nice being a teenager for these past eighteen years. But now the bit of adulthood is being forced upon us. It looks as though the time has come to take it between our perfectly straight teeth.

## WRAP SESSIONS

I went out to visit my parents at their cottage last weekend. Like so many summer places, theirs is furnished largely with discards from the house in the city. The furniture and small appliances were state-of-the-art twenty-five years ago, and as each of us grew up and moved away from home the contents of our bedrooms somehow gravitated lakeward.

In keeping with this decorating ethic, the reading materials are also quite outdated. This is all to the good because if they become sullied with sand or water or suntan oil it doesn't matter a whit to anyone; and currentness has never been important when it comes to summer reading. I was leafing through some brittle, sun-faded newsmagazine during this most recent cottage sojourn and came across an article about Christo, the Bulgarian artist who is often mistaken for a vegetable oil. He has somehow managed to make a living by wrapping landmarks, monuments, and bits of geography. Not content with having mummified art galleries, fountains, trees, and a whole chunk of the Australian coastline, Christo – at the time that article was written – was poised to wrap the Pont Neuf. He meant to use forty thousand square metres of shiny fabric. His aim in this enterprise was to make people think about the bridge differently. I don't doubt that he succeeded.

Certainly Christo deserved kudos for his chutzpah. Still, it's ironic that a man should find himself at the forefront of modern wrapping when for so many years it has been a folk art kept alive largely by women. Like quilters, wrappers have traditionally worked in the home, their efforts ignored by the media and taken for granted by their families. Now domestic wrapping is hovering on the edge of extinction. I didn't realize how serious the situation was until my mother and I went to the little grocery store near the cottage. Just inside the front entrance there was a display pyramid of Pampers disposable diapers that sparked off a chain of reminiscence.

"Pampers!" she said. "The women who buy those things don't know what they're missing."

"Mother," I said, "men buy them too, and I suspect they know exactly what they're missing. Surely you would have used them if they'd been around when we were toddlers."

"Oh, I'm not denying that the laundry was a nuisance. Why, at one point, I think I had all three of you in diapers at once. It was quite a chore. But all that folding and wrapping and pinning I went through had its rewards. It was even fun. I made a game of it. I'd pretend we were playing baseball and I was the team coach. The diaper was the baseball diamond and you were a player I was sending out for relief. Relief. That was my little joke. I'd plop you down, fold, tuck, and pin. Three strikes and you were out, all wrapped and ready to go. Why, I got so I could do it with one hand tied behind my back. Wrapping the perfect diaper left me with a small feeling of accomplishment. And besides, the repetitiveness, the mindlessness made it all quite soothing. It was sort of like meditation, I guess. So no, I don't think I would have been tempted to use disposable diapers. Not at all."

I'd never thought of the Zen of diapering before. I looked at my mother with new eyes. When we got to the kitchenware shelf of the store she scanned her list, muttering "Sandwich wrap, sandwich wrap."

I reached for some self-clinging cellophane.

"Not that!" she said, "I don't know where you get your ideas. What's wrong with good old wax paper? Your father and I never use that sticky stuff and we never did when you were growing up either."

It was true that cellophane was one of the miracles of modern chemistry that was an unknown quantity in our home. Other kids would pull Saran-wrapped delicacies out of their Munsters lunch buckets. I always carried a wax paper-shrouded sandwich in a paper bag. Back then I'd always thought this a little déclassé; but as I listened to my mother I understood how much care had gone into their wrapping.

"The trick was to get just enough paper, not too little, and above all not too much. If you tucked the corners under just so, the sandwich would lie flat as a waffle, and not even bulge through the bag. The best thing was that you couldn't see through it, so your lunch was always a surprise. These are the things a mother considers. I never wanted you kids to think your lunches were dull."

She had a point. I distinctly recall how the suspense of never knowing if my sandwich was peanut butter and jam or peanut butter and banana kept me on pins and needles all through elementary school.

"Besides," she continued, "wrapping all those sandwiches kept you in shape for Christmas." A dreamy look came over her then and I knew she was remembering Christmases past. I recalled what a dab hand she had been at wrapping the presents we got for our father. Back then, fathers received fairly predictable gifts: pipes, pen sets, tire pressure gauges. Mostly they came from the corner drugstore and they never had boxes. But my mother could wrap a pair of slippers so that they looked like a set of Reader's Digest Condensed Books. Even today I'm in awe of her skill.

We thought our separate thoughts as the checker tallied the groceries. When we got into the car, I noticed that my mother's eyes were damp. I knew she was mourning the loss of yet another tradition. I could feel the prickings of nascent guilt, for I have been unknowingly complicitous in this deterioration of wrapping skills. I don't have children but if I did, I would certainly cave in to the siren song of Pampers, and wouldn't spend my days washing diapers and trying to mask the odour of the pail they call home. I seldom take a lunch to work, but when I do I throw some sticky stuff around it, and have never in my adult life bought wax paper. And I always buy gifts from stores that will wrap them on the spot.

The next day, before I left the cottage for home, I made sure I left that old magazine article out where she would find it. I hope that she and wrappers everywhere will take heart at the news of Christo's projects, and cull from it the lesson that celebrity and recognition can be achieved through wrapping. I think that my mother will identify with Christo's craft and obsession and will sympathize with the plight of one whom some people call a complete nutter. My mother and all devotees of diapers and other remnants of the past know that every artist gets his share of bum wraps.

# PVI

At a barbecue last week I found myself in a group of people who'd all had exotic vacations. They'd either been whitewater rafting on the Ganges, or they'd motorcycled the whole length of the Great Wall of China, or they'd cycled across the Gobi desert while playing the complete works of Paganini on the sousaphone. When someone asked me what I'd done, I muttered "Oh. You know. Spent a week at the cottage with the in-laws." A collective yawn welled in everyone's throat. Someone managed a dry, "Oh, how nice. A quiet sort of holiday." I felt dismissed and dull.

This feeling persisted until the next day when I happened to be having lunch with a psychologist friend. She told me that what I had experienced was a common end-of-summer syndrome, called Post-Vacation Inadequacy, or PVI.

"PVI is particularly common among men of your age," she said.

"Oh, come on," I said, "surely this is just another one of those mythical conditions you women are forever trying to foist on us."

"Not at all. PVI among men has been well-documented. Women can experience it too, of course, but it's much rarer. Anyway, you don't need to worry. It won't last long, and you can cure it quickly if you can just manage to effect an attitudinal change. Remember, *you're* the one who's decided that your holiday was dull. *You're* the one who thinks you're inadequate. *You're* the one who has to change things around."

(This is one of the reasons I found psychology so unsatisfactory as a helping profession. Its practitioners are always trying to make their clients accept responsibility for their lives. I'd be so much more grateful to a counsellor who could help me find someone to blame.)

"How do I change things around?" I asked, grudgingly.

"It's simple. Just find some way of reshaping your thinking. Start seeing that holiday as something exciting and vital. Exotic. Dangerous, even."

"But it was just a week at the cottage!"

She shrugged. "Nobody said it wouldn't be a challenge. Try writing it out. That's often helpful."

So I did. Here is the distillation of the exercise. I reshaped my experience into a little essay I call:

## THE IN-LAWS IN SUMMER
*A Study in Natural History*

In late spring the in-laws leave their overheated smoky urban dens in answer to an ancient call. They make their way to their summering grounds, called cottages, cabins, or in some instances, trailer parks. These places look like the urban dens, except that there is a superabundance of insect life, and the dwellings are accessible only via narrow dirt paths.

Unlike many other species, in-laws maintain close contact with their offspring. The young, accompanied by their pelvic affiliates, will visit the summering grounds at least once a year, generally during a week when it will rain incessantly. How they manage to choose this pluvial period is as much a mystery as how swallows find their way back to Capistrano.

In-laws are notoriously territorial towards their young, and may act aggressively, even violently, towards the child's mate. A typical manifestation of this hostile behaviour is the assigning of separate rooms, or possibly the pitching of a one-person pup tent for the mate. Mates who persistently come between in-laws and their young may find their lives threatened. If sufficiently provoked, an in-law will charge. If this happens you can escape by climbing a tree. Any in-law sufficiently agile to follow can be frightened off with a whack across the snout. Remember though, if you do this, that a week is a long time to spend in a tree.

It has often been written that in-laws are attracted by open garbage. This is true in a psychic sense, and unless you want them snuffling around in the dead of night you would be well advised to keep your diary and financial statements under tight cover.

In-laws communicate with each other and with their own children through a series of winks and nods and in-jokes that are understood within the family unit but are completely unintelligible to outsiders. With a little practice, though, you can decipher a few of the more common grunts. These include: "What is it you do again for a living?" and "Whattaya mean you don't play bridge?" and, more rarely, "Wanna beer?" If an in-law chooses to address you it is best to smile broadly and answer monosyllabically. Betray no fear, for they can smell it. Keep your mind fixed on your objective: to maintain some kind of dignity and to get out of there alive. Always remember, thousands of others around the country are doing the same thing. Fully ninety percent of them will live to tell the tale. There's no reason you can't be among that number.

My psychologist friend was right. No sooner had I finished writing than I felt the great weight of PVI lift from my soul. I was a new man and I had a wonderful plan as well. I'm going to write a series of self-help pamphlets. The first will come out this fall. It's called "The Inlaws at Christmas." Look for it in better bookstores everywhere.

## RAIN DANCING

I had a letter from my Uncle Gus in Winnipeg today. It was the first unabashedly sunny morning we'd had in Vancouver in about six weeks. The long rains seemed to have abated at last. Somewhere the doves are cooing and gathering olive branches for their nests. I was lying on a chaise longue in the front yard, subjecting as much of my body as I decently could to the friendly ticklings of the sun, when Shelley the postwoman trotted up the walk. Later in the summer, mindful of the warnings of the ozone-sensitive scientists, I'll use powerful sunblocks and wear hats. But on the first sunny day of what used to be tanning season, I still think of Old Sol as the harbinger of benign rumours, rather than malignant tumours. And so I throw caution—and a good deal of my clothing—to the wind and offer myself up wholesale for barbecueing.

"You're starting to look a little pink up on top," said Shelley, "If I were you, I'd move into the shade to read this letter from your Uncle Gus."

There are some people who would resent getting such unsolicited advice, and still others who would be offended at the notion that their letter carrier keeps such close tabs on their correspondence, but Shelley has had this route for years, and the truth is that a letter from Uncle Gus is hard to miss. His distinctive style is evident even on the envelope. He addresses them with whatever he happens to have on hand, in this instance, a red crayon. And he's into recycling, too. This envelope (it was stuck together with masking tape) had started its life conveying the propaganda of a television evangelist. Uncle Gus is forever writing away to the preachers of the airwaves. Every Sunday he'll send out as many as forty requests for tracts, for tiny crosses, and for free pictures of Jesus. Once he even got a Garden of Gethsemane pop-up book. And he's started me on a collection of Saints and Apostles bubblegum cards, for which I'll be forever grateful.

"I suppose you'll want thirty-seven cents," I said to Shelley, noticing that Gus, apparently lacking a stamp, had drawn a picture of the queen in the upper right hand corner.

"I'll overlook it if you can scrape up a cup of coffee. And a muffin would be nice. Or some toast. I didn't have time for breakfast this morning."

We went into the house and I set the coffee works in motion. "White or whole wheat?" I asked

"Whole wheat, please."

I put two slices into the toaster. While the bread got the tan I was missing, and while Mr. Coffee sang his burbly tune, I opened the letter. A cunning picture of Jesus fell out. When you tilted it towards you, he would raise his hands to show you the stigmata, and under his feet would appear the words "GIVE GENEROUSLY." The letter itself was written on the back of some Oral Roberts stationery. Shelley went into the fridge to find the peach jam, and I launched into another wander through the surreal world of Uncle Gus.

Weeping Willows Home for Golden Agers,
Winnipeg, Manitoba
June 7, 1988

Hey there, Billy Boy!

I see on the news that you folks out there in Vancouver are building arks, while here on the prairies we're drinking dust. Why is this, anyway? Is this that greenhouse effect they keep talking about? Can we blame it on the feds? Things just haven't been the same since old Trudeau stepped down, that's for darn sure. I'll tell you, it's as dry here as I've seen it anytime since the great dustbowls of the thirties. Which reminds me, did you ever hear about the time I was single-handedly responsible for breaking that drought? Here's how it happened.

Your Aunt Adele and me had just got engaged, and she decided that I could use some polish in the social graces line. You know, use a hanky, not your sleeve, don't pick your teeth with your knife, that sort of thing. She figured that one way to sand down my rough edges would be to sign us up for these ballroom dancing classes. I was game, too. I always did cut a mean rug, although I wasn't too good on the compulsory figures. Freestyle has always been my strength.

These lessons were held at Ramon's School of Dance and Etiquette. You could learn dancing, or you could learn what fork to use when. I used to call it the "Eatin' Deportment Store," which Adele didn't think was funny at all. Ramon was this greasy little weasel of a fellow. Adele thought he was just the cat's whiskers but I didn't take to him one bit. He looked kind of like Randolph Scott with the Asian flu. He had this sickly yellow tint to his skin, and he always smelled like cheap cologne and Camels. Him and Adele got on real well, and I admit that I was more than a little jealous. She was a quick study in the dance department, and he'd always use her as his partner to demonstrate the steps. I'd watch them whirling around the dance floor and it would just stick in my craw. What made things worse was that I couldn't dance to save my life. I couldn't keep anything straight. I was mixing up my rhumba with my two step with my tango with my waltz. I was a disaster, Billy Boy, and every time I'd try to strut my stuff that slimy little Ramon would roll back his eyes and say "Caramba!" whatever the hell that means. There was about a dozen of us taking these classes, and luckily for me there was a gal called Eunice who came along to the classes with her husband Harold. They lived out of town a ways, out towards Portage La Prairie. Eunice was as clumsy as I was, but she had a real sense of humour about it. After a while, we just got so we'd stand to one side and laugh about it. That Harold was a real good sport. He never seemed to mind, and it was probably the salvation of his toes that he didn't have to dance with Eunice all the time.

Adele had signed us up for six weeks of lessons, and I'll tell you Billy Boy, at the end of that time, she'd have put that Irene Castle to shame. At the last class Harold and Eunice invited us all out to their farm for a picnic and a dance. There was a reserve quite close to where they lived, and three of the Indians had put together a little dance orchestra. Harold said that he'd ask them to come around and play.

"They're the greatest," said Harold. "Fiddle, drums, and guitar, that's all there is to it. But they can really swing! Why even Gus and Eunice will want to dance when they hear them." And everyone laughed. Especially Ramon.

I didn't want to go but Adele had her heart set on it. On the appointed day, off we drove, out of town and through the country. And it was dry! It hadn't rained for weeks and all the topsoil was blowing away. The dust was thick in the air when we got to Harold and Eunice's place.

For the first couple of hours I was just miserable. We were all outside on the brown lawn. You could hardly breathe for the dust and it was hot as blazes. That little dance group from the reserve was pretty good, I guess, but all the music sounded the same to me. Worst of all, Adele and that oily Ramon were dancing every dance. I was feeling lower by the minute. Eunice must have noticed how down in the dumps I was looking, because she came on over to me and said, "Here. Have a swig of this. You'll feel better." And she handed me this flask. "It's homemade," she said

Remember how we went to Mexico a few years ago, Billy Boy, on the Greyhound, and how we ate those peppers by mistake? I'll tell you, they were pablum compared to this hooch. It was like drinking battery acid. I thought the roof would come right off my mouth. I took one swallow. Then another. And then another. And suddenly everything was different. I saw the world with new eyes. I heard the music with new ears. There was a beat that went straight to my feet. And Billy Boy, I started to dance. I felt like a dervish in a blender. Everyone cleared out of my way. I had the whole lawn to myself. I heard Adele saying "Gus, what's wrong?" I heard Ramon saying "Caramba, he's loco." I didn't care. The Indian band stopped playing their waltzes and watched what I was doing. And they began to play a weird, thudding tune. They began to chant. Around and around I whirled, faster and faster. I felt a tremendous whoop rising in my throat. I let it fly, but it was drowned out by a huge clap of thunder, and the next thing I knew I was lying on the ground staring up at the sky, watching the lightning strut its stuff above me, and the rain was just gushing. And then I passed out.

I didn't wake up till hours later. They'd laid me out on the living room couch. The sun was coming out from behind the clouds, just in time to set. Water was running out the eaves. The first thing I saw was Adele, with a worried look on her face, sitting by my side. She gave me a big smile, and that was a sight for bloodshot eyes, I can tell you. Standing silently in the doorway to the room were the three players in that Indian band. The oldest of them came and sat down beside Adele. He looked at me, long and hard.

"That dance," he asked, "where did you learn that?"

"Beats me. It just happened in my feet."

"Thirty years ago my grandfather tried to teach me those same steps. But I wasn't interested in learning. I didn't want to have anything to do with the old ways. Now I see how powerful that dance is. Could you teach us?"

But you know, Billy Boy, I never could. It was lost history. Still, I figure if I did it once, I can do it again. All I need is the right circumstances, and the right stimulation. It's a long shot, I grant you. But remember that tequila I brought back from Mexico? I think I'm going to give it a go. Take care, kiddo. Regards to Shelley.

Affectionately,
Uncle Gus.

"Well how about that?" said Shelley.

"Don't you want to eat your toast?" I asked. It had popped up while I was reading.

"Nope," she said, looking at her watch. "Gotta run. I'm behind schedule now."

And off she jogged, her mailbag swinging, her can of dog repellant glistening in the sun.

## INFLATABLE TOYS

Sociologists, journalists, and other people who ask prying personal questions of complete strangers, tell us that the tragic emergence of AIDS as "disease of the century" has caused many people to shore up their love lives and eschew freewheeling frolicking in favour of what has come to be called "safe sex." It's ironic that this new era of restrained sexual practice has been attended by the most liberal discussions of sex ever seen in the popular media. Five years ago the now-commonplace news report allusions to condoms, semen, unprotected anal intercourse, and oral sex would have raised eyebrows, and probably hackles. However, it seems to have been recognized that the gravity of the problem merits a frank discussion.

In most places this effort to safeguard the health of the sexually-active populace has been welcomed. Canada, however, is a country that prides itself on its regionality, and predictably, local governments have not been unanimous in their praise of the educational direction taken by health officials.

British Columbia, for example, has the highest incidence of AIDS of any province in the country. Still, Premier Bill Vander Zalm spoke out fiercely against the open display and discussion of condoms in school classrooms. Instead, this father of four put himself forward as an advocate of celibacy, which is the only other fairly sure method of avoiding the spread of the disease.

Mr. Vander Zalm came under fire from so-called liberals and bleeding heart types who called his stance blinkered and narrow-minded. And yet I have evidence that he may be correct. Early exposure to condoms can lead to profligacy, and I am the living proof. Here is my story.

It's a hot summer day, the August before I start school. It's a time of green-leafed innocence. All is well with the world. They are dropping bombs in Nevada, but it is a long way away. Kennedy has not yet gone to Dallas. The Beatles are playing basements in Liverpool. The big star on Ed Sullivan is still Topo Gigio. On this hot, hot day, my mother has been making the furniture shine and smell like lemons. Now she is relaxing. She is sitting on the front steps with Stella, her best friend. They are chain smoking Matinée cigarettes and swilling black coffee. It is Winnipeg. It is summer. It is 1961.

I'm bored. Bored with the sandbox. Bored with my bicycle and its training wheels. Bored with opening the snapdragons to see if any bees are trapped inside. It's time for excitement. It's time for exploration. It's time to sneak into my parents' bedroom.

Oh, it's an Aladdin's cave of delights. Look! There's the closet, all dark and rustly and all full of mysterious musty smells. There are Mommy's high heels! She gets mad if you wear them, but I'll try them on anyway. She'll never know. I'll teeter across the room and back again. They sure are tricky! How does she walk in them anyway? Oh, let's bounce for a bit on Mommy and Daddy's great big bed, the one you get to crawl into when you've had a nightmare, and where you get to lie down and drink ginger ale as a special treat if you've had the flu. Over there is their dresser. On top is the pretty velvet box where Mommy keeps her jewels. Open it up. There's the brooch you bought for her last year at the Children's Bazaar. Why doesn't she ever wear it?

Right beside the jewel box is the little cedar box where Daddy keeps his handkerchiefs, and his cuff links too. Here is his sock and underwear drawer. Where is the funny pair of long underwear, the ones where the bum part unbuttons? There they are, right at the bottom! And look! What's this underneath? Balloons? Yes! Balloons! Oh, funny Daddy.

No sooner do I pick one up than evil thoughts run through my mind. The devil speaks in my ear. He says, "Bill." This is new. It's the first time the devil has used my name. "Bill," he says, "take that balloon to the bathroom. Fill it with water. See how big it can get. Wait for further instructions." I do what I'm told. The devil is right beside me. I can feel his heat. He gives me a jab with the fork he carries, just like he does in the comics. He says, "Bill, take that balloon upstairs and go to the window." I do.

The window is open. The air outside is hot and full of the low sounds of my mother's and Stella's voices on the steps below. The devil says, "Bill, take that balloon and throw it out the window." I do. The next sounds are the splattering of the ballon and the piercing cries below.

What happens next is a bit of a blur. Suffice it to say that these were the days when corporal punishment was still fashionable. The moral of the story is plain. Early exposure to condoms will undermine a child's moral values. I'm glad I was caught and punished. Had I got off free as a bird, I would probably have continued on the wayward, devil-led path. Probably I would be doing time even now, for breaking into safes.

## HAVING A NOVEL

**Ah**, the Labour Day long weekend! What a time of nostalgia. The dog days of summer are dozing in their kennel. The bald man in the elevator has stopped whistling *In the Good Old Summertime* and has taken up *Try to Remember the Kind of September.* Binders are being loaded with fresh sheaves of looseleaf. Listen! You can hear the sharp report of their three rings snapping shut. The odd frisbee may still scud on by. There are a few stubborn summer resurrectionists out in their backyards, igniting charcoal and mesquite. But even among the diehards there is an air of resignation. It's as though the world has heaved a collective sigh, and resolved itself to the inevitable turning of the page.

However, since the mid-seventies there has been a small but committed group of writers who have no time for this sort of wistful rumination. They spend their Labour Day weekends labouring: grunting, groaning, sweating, praying, heaving, sighing, regretting the foolish decision that has led them to a bed of exquisite pain. I refer to the participants in the annual three day novel-writing contest.

The contest has been sponsored each year by Pulp Press, an innovative publishing house based in Vancouver. The idea for the contest was born, as so many great ideas are, in a bar. Essentially, a bunch of drunken writers challenged each other to a literary duel: I dare you to write a novel in three days. Word of their enterprise got out and the idea caught on. Thousands of writers all over the continent now take part. The rules are simple. You can begin your novel anytime after midnight on the Friday of the Labour Day weekend. You must finish it by midnight, Monday. What you do between times is your own business. The completed novels are submitted to Pulp Press where, as a punishment for their initial cleverness, the editors have to read the mostly incoherent ramblings of sleep-deprived, first-time writers. The winning novel is published, and the author is put on public display on a coast-to-coast promotional tour.

I have had no fewer than two Labour Day weekend novels. I can say that each experience was unique, and that both irrevocably altered my life and my view of the world. I would like to pass on hints to those of you who are considering this transformative process of having a novel.

It is essential that you begin by putting your mind at rest. Look around you and you will see that more people are having novels now than at any time since the late forites. Indeed, we seem to be in the midst of a novel boom. How fortunate then, that despite the necessary discomfort, having a novel has never been as safe as it has become in our time. Do remember though, that every novel is unique, and no one else's experience will be exactly like your own. Some people manage to draw their novel forth with only the crudest of implements, and experience only minimal scarring. Others require the assistance of fancy electronic equipment, and are still torn asunder by the process, unseamed from the nave to the chops, as it were. You won't know your lot until you are well into the thick of it.

Despite the advances made in recent years in novel-having, there are still many myths and misconceptions surrounding the whole business. Everyone will have some sort of good advice to offer. Certain friends and relatives will try to push you into a process called natural writing. This involves refusing all pain killers, opening up as far as you can, and just letting the novel flow out of you. Many novelists begin this way, but find that after the second day of their labour they cannot refuse offers of scotch, cigarettes, and other relaxants. I took to these devices after the first hour. Each novelist must make his or her own choice.

Equally personal is the decision about where to have the novel. Many people prefer the security of a hotel or office space, where there is assistance readily available, and in many cases, specialized equipment that can be wheeled out in case of emergency. Still, more and more writers of all social strata are electing to have their novels at home, some even on the kitchen table. Whatever you decide, it is important that you have a group of supportive friends nearby, people to act as midwives to the muse. You may wish at times to be alone. You will not have bathed, brushed your teeth, or slept for some time. You will be more vulnerable than you have ever been and you will not feel attractive. But believe me, it is a huge help to have some coach nearby, someone to hold your hand in the final moments of pain, someone to tell you, "Push! Push! You're almost there!"

Prepare yourself for the "Is that all there is?" syndrome of post-novel depression. When your labour is finally over and you hold your novel in your hands, it may seem to you at first to be scrawny, ill-formed, weak, and wrinkled. Put your mind at ease. It's always like that. Until you have released your novel into the world, there's no telling what it might do. And remember that the first time is always the worst. It will seem like hell while you're going through it, and for a few days after. But before you know it, those sleepless nights of drinking, smoking, and chocolate-eating will be behind you. You'll have your figure back! The pain will be a thing of the past. You'll be itching to have another one. It's just nature's way of making sure that we'll keep on having novels.

Good luck novelists. Don't give a thought to those of us who are out there wringing the last drops from the summer. Your weekend labour will be an experience you'll never forget.

## WATCHING THE NATIONAL

*A Sort of Love Poem*

In the twenty-second hour of the long day's twenty-four,
When the clock emits ten open-throated gongs,
We slide beneath our comforter just like the night before,
And listen to that old familiar song:

" 'The National' – with so and so," proclaims that voice stentorian,
And bedrooms from Tofino to St. John
Leave off being pleasure domes, become hard news emporia:
"Not now, my love! 'The National' is on!"

A brassy brace of trumpets blat proud, heraldic huzzahs,
Computers in the background strum a chorus,
We're stuck fast in this moorage, safe in stormy seas because a
Steadfast Anchor fills the screen before us.

It's smiling Peter Mansbridge, heir to Knowlton's throne and sceptre.
His voice is firm, his manner calm and winning.
Balding men from coast to coast are Peter's earnest debtors:
He won the crown although his hair is thinning.

"Good evening," he intones and then he chants some incantation,
A spell to bring about his nightly magic
That whisks us from the coddled cots of this sub-Arctic nation
To territories torrid, torn, and tragic.

Our four walls can protect us from the chilly north wind's quaking,
Our roof fends off the rude rain's slurs and slander.
But small cracks in the seams give way to wholesale rents and
breaking
And we shiver at the Anchor's camera'd candor.

He has his finger on the pulse of West Beirut and Gaza,
He knows the real score in Nicaragua.
No scandal hides from his sharp eyes, in Panama he has a
Source for every sordid, secret saga.

And we, numb in our trundle bed, survey the marching Horrors
Wave their flags of terror, death, and harm.
We seek our solace from the nightly litany of terror
In the buildup of each others' arms.

Till once again that ton-of-bricks style message falls upon us:
That life is cheap and flesh will waste away.
We recollect the punchlines of those half-forgotten sonnets:
Gather rosebuds. Come, let's seize the day!

The Anchor reads an item of the "man bites dog" persuasion,
In which we're meant to find hope's withered kernel.
He says "Goodnight," and then invites folks all across the nation
To sit tight for the advent of "The Journal."

Not us. We've heard enough tonight, and Barbara Frum is banished
To the far-off limbo land of out of sight.
Our room's restored to us once more. The outer world has vanished.
Put out that lamp. It's time to seize the night.

## MARGARET LAURENCE

*"The Canadian and Soviet national teams were disqualified after a bench-clearing brawl . . ."*
–Globe and Mail, front page story, January 6, 1987

*"Margaret Laurence, one of Canada's most respected writers of fiction died yesterday at her home."*
–Globe and Mail, page 11, January 6, 1987

In each person's life there comes a time when he or she feels to be swimming against the prevailing current of the country. One of those upstream moments came on me because of a junior hockey brawl in Czechoslovakia, or rather because of the media attention lavished on the event. For me this incident had no more resonance than, say, a reported teenage gang fight on the streets of Penticton or Kiev. It meant nothing more to me than that a bunch of teenage boys, dedicated, athletic, and immature, fell prey to whatever instinctual or hormonal or patriotic impulses happened to be coursing through their brains at a given moment. It was astonishing to me that radio phone-in lines were jammed with responses to the incident. It amazed me that "The Journal" devoted almost twenty minutes to an analysis of why a lot of young men felt compelled to pummel each other on the ice of Prague. Why, I wanted to ask, has so much air time been given over to quizzing the returning players, to asking them hollow questions about why they did it when the answers are so transparent and predictable? Why all the mindless speculation about whether or not the nasty Soviets connived to provoke our boys into a mess that wasn't of their making?

I am not obtuse. I understand the pivotal role ice hockey plays in our culture. I have, over the years, observed how every subtlety and nuance and tremor of the game elicits some response from its many aficionados. I have come to wryly accept the certainty that when our dancers and musicians distinguish themselves in competition with performers from eastern bloc nations, they will receive scant attention and acclaim. I have thought from time to time that if dancers or pianists or writers were more given to acts of violence they might find themselves more frequently in front of the cameras or on the front pages of the papers. "ROYAL WINNIPEG TRASHES KIROV!" I can see it all now.

I probably wouldn't have thought twice about the coverage of the Prague set-to had it not been for the death of Margaret Laurence. In her writing, and in her life, she stood against everything that the hockey brawl represents. She stood for peace. She stood for morality. As a novelist she stood for a measured and introspective evaluation of a situation and an intelligent response to it. As a crusader against censorship she stood for the creation of strong and vital body of Canadian literature. She stood for courage. She stood for – dare I say it – Art.

It irritates me more than I can say that the loss of one of this country's greatest writers has been accorded less attention than the loss of a bronze medal by a teenage hockey team. Now, I never knew Margaret Laurence. She didn't seem like a very flashy person, and probably she wouldn't have wanted a sensational response to her private death. Perhaps she would have been offended by this quantitative response to her dying. All that is sure is the passing of time, and the certainty that her stories will shine on when the sad little hockey fight is a dim and tired tale.

# DOGWOOD

The tree my father turned into a dog was an oak, which was a commonplace tree on Hart Avenue. But the species chosen by the landscape architect who had designed our subdivision never achieved the glory implicit in that name. Oak: the many ringed, thick trunked and lordly trees of Sherwood, O dark and brooding sacred gathering place of the Druids. This was not for Hart Avenue. Ours were gaunt and craggy oaks that grew tall but not wide, trees whose rasping bark was flecked by a feathery, orange moss.

They weren't very useful trees. Their branches would never be sufficiently sturdy, nor appropriately spaced to accommodate a tree house. They provided only inconsequential shade from the summer sun: perhaps enough to shelter a very thin child and a very small lemonade stand, or for a dog to find some sort of tongue-lolling comfort during the hottest part of the day. In the fall the oaks up and down the street all shed a quantity of brown leaves that seemed wholly disproportionate to the degree of protection they had afforded during their greener lifetimes. The leaves were a chore-making annoyance. At the same time though, a feeling of happy community fell over Hart Avenue on that Saturday morning late in September when, through instinct, everyone went to the basement or backyard shed and excavated the rake. This was in the days before the advent of green plastic garbage bags, before city officials in a magnanimous show of concern for our pulmonary well-being forbade the burning of leaves. This was well before Les Thornton next door died of the hiccups, before baby Paul across the street traded in his Beverly Hillbillies lunchbucket for an electric guitar and a Mohawk. This was before Mrs. Wingrave decided that seventy-three was not too old to learn the harmonica and did, and then one summer evening after one too many gin and tonics stood at the top of her steps playing "Old Folks at Home" with nothing on, and someone called the police and after that she went away to live with her daughter.

The raking of leaves always took longer than was strictly necessary. A one hour sweep-up would have been sufficient for their simple gathering, but more time was needed to explore their possibilities. Leaves could be picked up and thrown, leaves could be piled and then jumped in, again and again, until parental tempers ran thin, and the dross of the oaks was gathered into cardboard boxes and taken to backyard incinerators to be turned into gold.

The oaks also produced a goodly quantity of acorns. Some acorns were conscientiously left behind for the squirrels. Many would be gathered up with the leaves as bonfire food. They made satisfying popping sounds in the flames. Myths had grown up around the acorns. One was said to have exploded in a fire a few streets over and the flying shell blinded someone. Acorns were thought to be poisonous to humans, just like the mysterious purple berries that grew on the nameless shrubs everyone had planted to mask the jutting hot air vents from their dryers. Every year, as a kind of rite of passage, a few of the bigger boys, who only the year before stood back away from the fire for fear of wearing an eye patch for the rest of their days, would peel back the shell from the acorn and eat the rosy-veined, peach colored meat. When immediate death did not result from this daring, some other danger would be found.

"Holy geez, didja see the size of the worm hangin' outta that one that Kenny ate? Dintcha see it Kenny? It was hardly that big! I know a kid who ate a worm like that once and a few nights later he woke up 'cause he couldn't breathe 'cause the worm had crawled up from his stomach and into his nose."

Those were hazy afternoons on Hart Avenue. The leaves turned into aromatic ghosts. Women blew smoke rings and waved to each other from doorways. Men leaned on their rakes and addressed laconic remarks to their neighbours, grunt-like utterances issued from behind pipestem-clenching teeth. The younger children, those who wouldn't yet dare to swallow an acorn, tugged at their fathers' pant legs, begging for an acorn pipe. These were crafted by lopping the top off an acorn with a pen knife, cutting out the meat and preserving the shell. When a small twig was inserted into the bottom of the bowl as a stem, the result was a dandy pipe.

My father carved the best acorn pipes on Hart Avenue, a fact acknowledged even by the conceited Lorelei who lived down the street. Other fathers, well meaning but maladroit, turned out a product that was scarcely a notch above what had been given them by nature. My father made art. He would scrape away the nut so carefully and thoroughly that only a porcelain-thin and eggshell-light skin remained. Working quickly and delicately, he would score the casing so that the bowl was rough textured, like a corncob pipe. Perhaps he would engrave a small heart, or a diamond or a four leaf clover on it. "It's just whittling," he would say dismissively when he handed us the finished pipe.

My father, a banker, had always "just whittled." He carved a seagull perched on a rock, its wide wings spread, its beak clamped onto a fish. He carved a heron, spindly-legged against rushes. He carved an Indian head from a photograph by Edward Curtis. Birds or Indians, he always worked from photographs. The time he turned the oak into a dog was the only time he ever worked from life. The dog was Mitchell, our mongrel, who looked as much like a springer spaniel as he looked like anything. My father turned him into oak at the tag end of the dog's life, when Mitchell was half blind and too tired out to be anything but a complacent model. In palmier days, when he had been a thin-blooded, handsome dog around town, Mitch had led a colourful life. He had bitten both the postman and our minister. He was a playboy who carried on his romantic intrigues in the school yard. I never knew when I might look from my classroom window and see him frolicking disgracefully with Muffin, with Sheba, and once, with Rinty.

"Isn't Rinty a boy dog?" I asked my mother that day after school.

"I believe so," she answered. "Why?"

"No reason."

For where would I find the words to tell her what I had seen?

The oak that became Mitchell was one of two in our front yard. It had become diseased and needed to be removed. The operation left behind a stump that stood about eight feet tall. It was unsightly, and the sensible thing would have been to remove it altogether, and plant in its stead a silver maple, which would have been patriotic; or a lilac, which would have been fragrant; or an elm, which would have been shortsighted, given the Dutch elm blight that was soon to sneak onto Hart Avenue.

But my father saw with the presumptive eye of the sculptor. It was his small vanity to believe that he could see into the heart of wood and find revealed there the true nature and ambitions of insentient matter. For him, wood was never sufficient unto itself. It was a dark prison where some hidden form lay in bondage. His was the mission of the liberator, and through the tightly circled rings of the stump of the oak he saw Mitchell struggling to be free.

The oak came down in the spring, and all that summer—Mitchell's last dog days—my father worked. He stripped off the bark from the corpsey trunk, turning it into a column, a pedestal on which Mitchell would perch for something like eternity. Mitchell himself, antique and doddering, destined in the winter to be dispatched to meet his maker through the chemical mercies of the veterinarian, was insensible to his immortalization. He spent that whole season of his sculpting in a happy green stupor on the grass, enjoying whatever smells came his way, but too wise and exhausted to do anything about them. The new generation of squirrels—who must certainly have heard tales of the fearsome beast from their beleaguered parents—were given every reason to wonder at the caveats of their elders. It was not true that this dog would chase them mercilessly, and bark threats as they ran along the telephone wires. No, they could frolic undisturbed under his very nose if they cared to. And they did. The cat across the street, whose life he had made a misery for a dozen years, came to understand that her old foe was a menace no longer. Time had been kinder to her, a fact she never tired of flaunting by stalking birds in plain view of God and Mitchell, neither of whom thought it worth the trouble to strike her down. Muffin, Sheba, and Rinty had died or left Hart Avenue years before, but had one of them somehow appeared and tried to entice Mitchell back to the schoolyard with erotic blandishments, he would have regarded them with rheumy eyes, grinned a doggy grin of fond recall, and drifted back to sleep.

"Whatcha up to, Stan?" asked the neighbours as my father stood on his stepladder, chisel in one hand and mallet in the other.

"Whittling. Just whittling."

"Well, what's it going to be, Stan? Totem pole or something?"
"Nope. Dog."
"Oh. That'll be nice then, won't it. Good luck, Stan."
The stump of the oak measured about thirty inches in diameter. Given these dimensions, it would have been impossible to carve the dog as he was, all placid and supine. Both the width of the tree, and my father's sense of artistic purpose dictated that Mitchell's permanent posture should be more dignified. Bit by bit, chips of the stump were knocked away to reveal a sitting dog, his back straight, his profile patrician, his spaniel ears long and silky, his waistcoat feathered.
"Why, that's Mitchell. It certainly is," exclaimed Mrs. Woolman, whose cancer was still only a small twinge, but who would not see another spring.
"What a talent you have, Stan," said the newly widowed Mrs. Thornton who was soon to move to Calgary.
What the neighbours said privately, I have no idea. Perhaps it did not strike them as unusual or eccentric that a man would carve a dog out of a tree in the front yard. Perhaps they didn't mind that the traffic picked up on quiet Hart Avenue as word of the dog carver got out and people drove by in the evening to study the sculptor's progress. Perhaps they were genuinely delighted to learn of my father's talents. Certainly they were surprised. He had always kept his whittling a private business, apart from the acorn pipes. By the time he turned the oak into a dog, our childish delight at these had been supplanted by more grown-up enthusiasms.
Looking back, I'm suprised that my father wasn't nonplussed by the attention he received that summer. He was then, and still is, a solitary and undemonstrative sort. Perhaps, in his way, he was really making a public statement. Not a boast, but a simple declaration. "Look. You think I am a man who works in a bank, a pleasant man of few words. But here is what I truly am, a man who sees into the heart of wood."
The summer passed, the chisel chipped, and by the time the remaining oaks had spilled their leaves, both Mitchells were almost done. Early in the winter, my father picked up the dog from the slippery kitchen linoleum where he had fallen one too many times, and carried him out past his oaken likeness to the car. When he came home, he phoned in sick to work, made some tea and sat all day

quietly in his chair. He didn't carve anything all the rest of that season. In January, when the prairie weather was bitter, he put a woolen toque on the wooden dog. In the spring he found an eagle imprisoned in a block of walnut, and went back to whittling.

# OTHER NONS

I would be the last person in the world to call into question the righteousness or the worthiness of this country's vocal anti-smoking lobby. They have filled their rose-pink lungs with smoke-free air and broadcast their message near and far. Only a fool would suggest that we are all not the better for it. My only quibble with the pure airists is that they, with the exuberance of their beliefs, have clouded the efforts of other special interest groups who wish to make their cases publicly known. Let us consider then, for a few brief moments, the ideologies of some of society's less celebrated Nons.

There is a substantial faction out there, and I confess I am among them, who believe that the world would be a superior place if the facilitators of comfort in airplanes or in restaurants made available not just smoking and non-smoking sections, but also witty and non-witty ghettoes. After all, no matter how great a regard one has for another's privacy, there are times when it is impossible to avoid being privy to some other group's conversation. How annoying this can be if their talk is offensive! But, if witty and non-witty seating arrangements could be made, all discomfort might be circumvented. People bent on having discussions about denture adhesives, free trade, weight control, aphids, gall bladders, Mila Mulroney, zucchini bread and Joan Collins could all carry on, free of the worry that they would be disturbed by Oscar Wilde sound-alikes. Such people, as we all know, are trenchant, cutting, abrasive, biting, flip, sarcastic, and aphorisitc. Really! If they must sparkle in public, then surely they should do it where others won't be put upon by their frippery.

Yet another distinction that might well be made is that of garlic and non-garlic. Putting these two breeds together is simply asking for trouble. Non-garlics are especially strong-minded and cannot abide the folkloric notions expounded by their opposites; notions that suggest that garlic is life-prolonging, and in fact, has aphrodisiac qualities. "Rubbish," cry the opponents of the pungent bulb. Their gospel has it that garlic's only property is to lend a none-too-subtle ethnic air to its adherents. This is patently offensive to non-garlics, who tend to smell slightly of Scotch mints. In an informal survey I conducted I also discovered that non-garlics tend to prefer Florida to Florence, Mickey Mouse to Michelangelo, galoshes to Guccis, and Gouda to Gorgonzola. Non-garlics by and large hold opposing views to pro-garlics on such vital issues as nuclear disarmament, the ozone layer, and the shroud of Turin. Furthermore, study after study has shown that the garlic habit is acquired largely through example, and that it is only a short step to the ingestion of other noxious substances, such as marinated squid. Surely it is time the rights of non-garlics were recognized!

Yet another unsung source of social divisiveness is child disciplinarian vs. non-child disciplinarian. Why should a non-disciplinarian be compelled to sit in a restaurant and watch other parents force their progeny to wear the dreadful, scarring shackles of manners, of courtesy? How loathsome it is for a non-disciplinarian to see a child forced to say please, or thank you; how upsetting to see a youngster made to chew with its mouth closed, to abstain from drinking from the ketchup bottle. Mixing the disciplinarian with the non-disciplinarian is to invite confrontation, and should not be undertaken unless you have direct access to a UN peacekeeping force.

There are countless other Pros and Nons out there, battling for the plum of social approbation. We have Spandex and non-Spandex; Jane Fonda Workout and non-Jane Fonda Workout; Masterpiece Theatre and non-Masterpiece Theatre; Stephen King and non-Stephen King; Allergic and non-Allergic; Joan Rivers and non-Joan Rivers; Likes to Hear Every Detail About a Cesarean Section and non-Likes to Hear Every Detail About a Cesarean Section. I could go on, but I'm sure you get the idea. Just thinking about the shocking inequities out there has made me so angry that I've decided that something radical has to be done to wake up the public service sector to the needs of society's many nons. I've opted for the course of direct and obnoxious action. You'll know me when you see me. I'll be the one sitting in a restaurant, smoking Camels, reading Noel Coward out loud, ordering more garlic bread and hissing at young children. Don't bother stopping to thank me. I'm just doing my part.

## GRAND AND UPRIGHT

Those of us who are vocationally underused, if not absolutely unemployed, know that the worst of our condition is the cruel imbalance in the availability ratio of time to money. One has scads of one and none of the other, and it sadly seems that never the twain shall meet. Anyone who has been in this position understands the never-ending challenge of devising a life system that accommodates the dictates of both style and economics. Why, just going for coffee can be a problem when a mere mug of java can set you back two dollars, at least if you prefer to swill the stuff in those tony bistros where one cares to be seen.

Latterly I have learned that a good place to cadge a free cup of coffee in pleasant surroundings is in those opulent hotels that host large conferences. If you look prepossessed and self-confident you can stroll right past the supercilious desk staff and into the conference area, where there is always a glistening urn all ready and primed to accommodate the needs of dozy conferees. If you go early in the morning you can score some tasty muffins and a Danish. Later in the day there is sometimes a host bar and tiny but succulent hors d'oeuvres.

I've done this more often than I care to confess. I have rubbed shoulders with anthropologists and engineers, with teachers and with many species of trade unionists. At times I have even slipped into some of their sessions and learned about the challenges facing the members of professions with which I have no affiliation whatsoever. I recommend this to anyone. It can be very broadening.

Just the other week I stumbled on a most entertaining conference. It was a joint meeting of the American Musicological Society, the College Music Society, the Ethnomusicological Society, and the Society for Music Theory. On the first day of their conference I picked up a copy of their agenda. Rarely have I been privy to the evidence of such erudition. It was immediately clear to me that this conference would be fairly exploding with pyrotechnic displays of scholarly prowess. Among the papers to be presented were: "Improvisation and the Performer-Composer in Courts, Temples, and Brothels," "The Mescalero Apache Girls' Puberty Ceremony: a Consideration of the Role of Music in Structuring Ritual Time and Transformation," "Stylistic Environment and the Scat Singing Style of Ella Fitzgerald and Sarah Vaughan."

I sat down in one of the hotel's plush loveseats and watched the legitimate conferees bustle into their various sessions. How amazing, I thought, that anyone who begins music lessons as a child starts out on the same flat plane of ignorance, but that some take those first tentative flirtations with the piano or the accordion or the violin and turn them into passionate affairs—affairs that drive them to scale such craggy, hoary summits as "Social Dance Music in Malay Villages and Courts: Its Performance, Its History, and Its Sexuality."

With such mind-nourishing fare available to them, I knew that these scholar-musicians would have no interest in the sort of junk-food contributions I might offer them. Still, it seemed only fair to come up with some sort of recompense for the cups of coffee to which I would certainly help myself. And so I scooped up a couple of the note pads and pens that had been provided (as well as a lemon Danish—the apple had been so tasty) and drafted this modest paper. It is called:

## GRAND AND UPRIGHT
### *The Piano as a Tool for Rite of Passage*

Our piano arrived on one of those amber-hued late August days in Winnipeg. It was 1963. We had bought the piano from a Presbyterian Church. A room in our house had been readied for it. My brothers and I watched, amazed and wide-eyed, as the four sweaty rent-a-brutes who had been engaged for the occasion humped it down the narrow hallway, risking catastrophe at every step. We waited, all brimming with glee and dread, for the sound of rending wallpaper or splintering bone. We felt as though we were receiving a visit from a legendary, imposing, and immobile great aunt.

The piano was stiff, upright, and set in its ways. When its mouth was opened we saw a row of chipped and yellow teeth. Once it had been handsome. Now—just as a great aunt might—it bore the scuffs and bruises and outward signs of the disappointments of its strict Presbyterian past. Once it was installed, there was no question but that room now belonged to it, and it alone. It took over straight away, this hulking amalgam of tree and elephant. We wanted to prod it directly, to provoke it into telling us whatever stories it might know. But my mother closed the door on it.

"Leave it alone now. Dad will know what to do about it when he comes home."

That night after dinner, my father went down to the basement and emerged with a box full of dampish, mildew-smelling sheet music. We had never known it was down there, never known that he had played when he was a young man. This music introduced me to a fragment of the not-so-distant past of which I had known nothing. Here was a song called "Always," with a cover photograph showing the doe-eyed Deanna Durbin. ("She was from Winnipeg, you know," said my mother. This made me gape. It had never occurred to me that anyone famous could come from Winnipeg!) Here was leggy Betty Grable on the arm of Harry James. There were the Andrews Sisters and Eddie Cantor. There were names like Jack Benny, Irving Berlin, Cole Porter, and Noel Coward.

As they sifted through these treasures, my mother and father would release little coos of nostalgia. I understood for the first time that there was more to their histories than I had ever suspected. Would musicologists believe that it was the piano and the promise of its singing that pulled me finally from the self-absorbed, narcissistic world of early childhood and into the knowledge that the world was very old before I was begun? (And if it didn't begin with me, it wouldn't end with me either. Well! There was a can of worms!)But these existential gnawings didn't last long. When my father sat down on the stool (which would give us many dizzy, happy hours of riding up and down), adjusted it to his height, played a few rolling chords, then launched into "Believe me if all those endearing young charms . . .", I could only think of how much I wanted to speak that mysterious language of clustered notes and lines.

I would guess that many of the scholars who sat in the hotel meeting room, hanging on every word of "Thumri and the Decline of the Courtesans," began their careers with lessons given by a neighbour lady who taught in a musty basement or a knick-knack littered living room. I had my first lessons in the elementary school gymnasium on Tuesdays at 4:30. This was a group session. Half a dozen of us were tutored by a woman called

Mrs. Gillette. (Her name was unfortunate. It used to be our delight to phone her in the evening and ask "Are your razors sharp?") On our first day we clustered about the flesh-toned school piano and were initiated into the mysteries of middle "C" and quarter, whole, and half notes. She told us too about the Toronto Conservatory, the awesome temple which would judge us at the end of the year. I gathered from her description that it was a fearsome and peripatetic inquisition, bent on searching out faults and condemning those it found lacking. I practised hard from week to week. I was determined that I would be found flawless in the eyes of my examiners.

We worked from a series of books that were written by an indefatigable someone named Leila Fletcher. Was Leila Fletcher a real person, or was she some sort of corporate invention like Betty Crocker? As a young student, I came to think of her as a kind of grandmotherly figure who stood at my elbow and whispered kind words of encouragement and advised patience.

I was overjoyed (and knew Leila would be, too) when I was finally allowed to use both the right and the left hands together. I learned by heart a seductive song called "Little Birch Canoe." I can now recall only the deathless line: "My little brother calls Yahoo!, I take him with me too." "Little Birch Canoe" became my party piece. I performed it for our Year End Recital. I trotted it out for the Toronto tribunal when they made their promised appearance. And I must have been adequate, for I was allowed to go on to Mrs. Gillette's second year class.

What befell me in that second year, I wonder, after such a promising start? What quality of being set me apart from the assembled musicologists who must, for the most part, have the Moonlights and the Appasionatas and the Chopin Polonaises living in their fingertips? The second year for me was the beginning of the end. We moved from the white keys onto the weepy sounding black ones. We were given a new book which contained works of the great composers in a somewhat diluted form. The book also contained their capsule biographies. The musicologists would snicker at those little histories, chockablock as they were with the kinds of apocryphal snippets that so appeal to children. I remember their stories as relentlessly sad. J.S. Bach was said to have gone blind from copying music by moonlight. Beethoven's terrible deafness was amplified in my ears. Mozart was buried in an unmarked pauper's grave. Schumann was a lunatic. Tchaikovsky drank unboiled water in unsanitary Russia and died of cholera.

Perhaps I apprehended from all this that a musical career led to nothing but grief, and that I would be well-advised to quit while I was ahead. It's more likely though that I just didn't have the gumption and wherewithal to stick with it once the pieces started getting difficult. I hated the look of key signatures with more than two sharps or flats, and the idea of compound time was one I would never grasp. I returned time and time again to the comforting familiarity of "Little Birch Canoe." I spent more and more time daydreaming about the tragic lives of the composers. Finally, when I stopped practising altogether, the lessons came to an end.

"If you're not going to use that piano, we'll get rid of it," my parents would say. I never took these threats any more seriously than their periodic suggestions that we might all be sent away to St. John's School for Boys, where it was said the instructors had licence to beat you, and where you could roll the pancakes into little balls and bounce them from floor to ceiling. One day though, I came home from school and found that the piano had been spirited away.

"Since you were no longer interested," said my mother lightly, "we decided to give it to the church." Not to the Presbyterians, mind, but to the United Church, our church. For all I know, it's there to this day, accompanying Sunday School choirs, and having medicine balls chucked into it by out-of-control Boy Scouts.

I long ago forgave my parents for this treachery, but oh, I was bitter on that day! It made no difference that I had been amply warned. I simply couldn't understand what possible satisfaction–other than that of petty revenge–they could derive from giving the thing away. At that very moment I had one of those small epiphanies that punctuate a life. I understood all at once that they and I were entirely different breeds. I did not then, and do not now, think that something stops being useful when it is no longer used. Even if the piano was silent, it had filled a space that now was vacant and might be occupied by any one of a number of visiting great aunts. And I had loved it, loved it for itself, for its brownness, its golden scroll of a name, and its unsung possibilities.

But all this was years ago. I shall put my residual resentments away and thank the piano for the things it taught me. Not that I can talk about "Ostinato Technique and Sonata Form in Schubert," but about the limits of skill, and the hidden histories of families, and about the tragic lives of geniuses. And I learned "Little Birch Canoe," which to this day is the only piano piece in my repertoire.

It saddens me that even though I hung around that musicological conference for four days and drank a vat of coffee, nobody asked me to play.

# KIDS BIDS

I have always been intrigued by the language and lore of children. I am fascinated by the resilient and persistent intelligence network that exists among them by which they have passed along their games and songs from Roman times until now. The enduring quality of youngsters' games has been amply documented by the English folklorists Peter and Iona Opie, and I have collected my own evidence to support their findings. The children who play in the schoolyard next to our house sing the same ritual songs we sang in Winnipeg. Even as I write, I can hear their high-pitched, penetrating, impossible-to-escape, delightful little voices bellowing:

Cinderella, dressed in yella
Went upstairs to kiss a fella
Made a mistake
Kissed a snake
How many doctors did it take?

I suppose it's possible that today's more savvy children chant this with a more conscious understanding of its phallic implications, but that is the stuff of a whole other examination.

I have also remarked that while many of these games and songs are virtually identical to those I knew many years ago, others betray some interesting regional differences. This is especially true of rhymes that are attached to special occasions. Take Hallowe'en for instance. On the west coast, children go from door to door and call out "Trick or Treat!" In Winnipeg, we knew of the trick-or-treat cult, but to us it made little sense. The use of the word *or* implied that there was an option; that one was seriously prepared to consider that the prospect of playing some cheap and nasty trick was as worthwhile as receiving a treat. My colleagues and I considered this notion both ludicrous and dishonest. Our preferred call was "Hallowe'en Apples." It had a little tune that went along with it. It looks like this:

Our Hallowe'en night calling card left no doubt that food was the object of the exercise. It was true, of course, that most of us aspired to something grander than apples: something in the chocolate line, perhaps. Maybe an Oh Henry! or a Milky Way. But even the lowly apple was preferable to that most ubiquitous of handouts, the candy kiss. These jaw-breaking bits of nastiness, all wrapped up in their orange and black paper, were the devil's own inedible invention. They were every bit as welcome as the kisses that lurked on the withered lips of great aunts, waiting to leap out and ambush unsuspecting young cheeks at Christmas time. (As I recollect, in fact, the much-scorned candy kisses were still around when those Yuletide smooches were bestowed. They would still be in the bottom of the pillow case that had been seconded for the collection of treats, growing all lumpen and mouldy.)

If Hallowe'en candy could be assigned monetary denominations, the candy kiss would be the grubby penny; the apple would be the dime; the little box of raisins would be the quarter; and the Oh Henry! would be the fifty cent piece. And the dollar? Ah, the pack of potato chips – that would be the dollar.

Stock in potato chips was so high because they were such a rare commodity. There was only one household in our neighbourhood where they were available. It was rumoured that the philanthropic soul who distributed them worked for the Old Dutch Potato Chip Company and so was able to secure these wares for a mere song. Now, every Hallowe'en Appler wanted to know the location of that house. There was an unspoken understanding, a childhood law, that once you found out you told no one. It was to be a hermetic secret, known only to initiates. If you wanted to acquire that sort of wisdom, you had to be prepared to work for it. To simply give it away would strip it of its magic. I was close to the end of my Hallowe'en career before I discovered the potato chip house. Of course, I was overjoyed. I felt like Galahad, finally grasping the elusive Grail. And at the moment those potato chips fell into my sack, a terrible idea leapt in my brain. I memorized that house number and began to connive.

My plot had to do with a television programme called "Kids Bids". (This was the Winnipeg appellation of the show; I believe it had other incarnations across the country.) It used to run on Saturdays, before "Bugs Bunny" and after the "Wide World Of Sports." "Kids Bids" was a kind of game show for little folk, sponsored by Old Dutch Potato Chips. Anyone who cared to collect masses and masses of chip packages and box tops could play. Each of these greasy tokens was worth a certain number of Old Dutch points. When you had a sufficient number of Old Dutch points you could go on the show and bid them against a whole bunch of swell prizes: transistor radios, Barbie dolls, Beatles albums, bicycles.

These prizes were pedestrian and didn't appeal to me in the slightest. The idea of being on television, however, did. Others of my contemporaries had been cute enough to be on "Romper Room," gifted enough to be on "Tiny Talent Time," some were in training for "Reach for the Top," and precocious Ina Gustafson was able to lie about her age and penetrate the bastion of "Teen Dance Party." None of these accomplishments were within my grasp. "Kids Bids" was another matter. Even I could collect potato chip packages, and wouldn't it be easier if I could get others to do the dirty work for me?

My friends with "Kids Bids" aspirations would spend their summers hanging around the shopping centre and other public places, rooting through the trash bins in search of point-winning packs. I didn't bother. For one thing my sensibilities were far too delicate, and for another, I had my master plan to put into effect. If I played my cards right I would have enough points by the first week in November to legitimately get into the studio, if not take away some trophy.

Early in October I leaked word that I knew the whereabouts of the potato chip house. I volunteered my services as guide to those who had not yet discovered it. I would be like Moses, leading the chosen people to a land, if not of milk and honey, then of starch and salt. All I asked in exchange was that my flock turn their potato chip packs over to me.

The grapevine buzzed with word of my proposal. The electricity of expectation buzzed through the late October air. On Hallowe'en night, I assembled my minions around me. I led them through the Red Sea right up to the fabled door. There, with one clamorous voice, we called out: "HALLOWE'EN APPLES!"

A plump hausfrau answered. She exclaimed at our numbers, and then sowed our pillow cases with handful after handful of the repulsive candy kisses. I can only suppose that the potato chip people had moved.

Oh, the bitter, scornful silence that fell over us as she shut the door! It seemed to go on forever. And then some of my disciples said some very unkind things before they scattered off in a thousand directions in search of more fertile ground. I was shunned for weeks afterward.

It was a just and fitting punishment. In boasting of my knowledge, and in volunteering to sell it, I had broken a childhood taboo. My reputation was besmirched. It was my last Hallowe'en. The paltry few potato chip packs that I had managed to collect by more honest means sat in a box under my bed until the spring when my mother threw them out, along with the last of the candy kisses. I didn't care. "Kids Bids" had lost its allure.

Legends die hard, as those school yard chants demonstrate. Probably there are still kids out there who go on a quest each year for the fabled potato chip house. Perhaps one day, they'll find it. But hear me, oh ye children, and learn from my sad lesson. If you figure out where to find those chips on the old block . . . keep it to yourself.

# RIVERDALE, NORTH

Every November for the past few years, one week has been set aside and designated as the Canadian Children's Book Festival. All across the country, authors and illustrators of Canadian children's books shunt from city to city, town to town, school to school and library to library, to read from their work and talk about the precarious business of wringing a living from the book business in Canada.

In the dim, dark, comic book strewn past of my own childhood such a thing as a Canadian Children's Book Festival would have been hard to imagine. Apart from *Beautiful Joe*, and the *Green Gable* books, Ernest Thompson Seton, and a few stories about rugged boys getting misplaced in the wilderness, there just wasn't a substantial body of domestic writing for young people. And there certainly weren't today's activist librarians, teachers, and booksellers; professional educators who take an advocacy position towards our national literature, who actively promote the idea of reading Canadian books. Had this been the case I would doubtless have become an entirely different, substantially superior brand of adult. However, with no one to lead me to purer water, I drank from the fetid stream of American comic books.

I blush to confess that I did not even read the socially redemptive, morally uplifting Junior Classics, which presented in highly diluted form the works of Hugo, or Stevenson, or Dickens, or Dumas. No, I read Richie Rich, Little Lulu, and most particularly, Archie comics.

How I loved those kids from Riverdale! When I was eight or nine years old they were sirens beckoning me towards the lotus-scented domain of teenhood. I wanted to be one of that gang. I wanted to know first hand Reggie's villainy, Jughead's goofiness, Archie's haplessness. I was charmed by Betty's unflagging goodness, intrigued by Veronica's money-fed narcissism. How many other little boys were led, like me, into their first deliberations on the Nature/Art conflict through their contemplation of the perfect topography of those two girls' sweaters?

But what I loved most about those comics was the mail order page. It was the source of the rarest treasures. There were whoopee cushions, and squirting boutonnieres, and pieces of moulded plastic craftily devised to resemble bits of canine unpleasantness. (The advertisement for this latter item featured an illustration of the startled expression that would cross the face of Everymother when she found Fido's foul forget-me-not on her best bedspread. What fun!) There were kits for growing coral gardens. There were tiny dogs that fit inside tea cups. There were muscle building machines. Best of all, there was a jujitsu manual, the possession of which guaranteed that you need fear no man.

I found this an attractive idea for I lived my life in a state of constant fear. I was one of those wimpy children, pathetic and bedraggled, the kind of child who by some Darwinian law is the easy and natural prey of bigger animals. Ever since the second grade I had been the property of a bully named Cameron. Cameron did everything he possibly could to make my life a trial. Had I been force-fed great works of literature – Canadian or otherwise – from an early age, I wouldn't have been so troubled by this. I would have understood that there were sociological or familial reasons for his brutish nastiness. I would have known that he was more to be pitied than scorned and feared. When he had me in a painful armlock, or when he had dumped me yet again head first into a prairie snow drift, I would have simply called to mind the words of Job or Boethius or even Farley Mowat, and just got on with my life.

However, as I've pointed out, this was not the case. My view of the world was informed by the simple morality of comics, where good would somehow, through perseverance, stealth, and the co-operation of the universe, triumph over evil. I saw the jujitsu manual as a way of hastening that process.

In June, at the end of the fourth grade, I clipped the coupon from an Archie comic, put it in an envelope along with the two dollars I had so painstakingly saved and sent it across the border. They were Canadian dollars, of course, for what did I know of exchange rates or international money orders? The ad cautioned that three weeks were required for delivery. I passed the time by preparing myself as best I could by studying the martial arts skills of Emma Peel on "The Avengers," and Cato on "The Green Hornet." They tossed imposing pugilists into the air as easily as if they had been rag dolls. I would send myself off to sleep by imagining the look of horror on Cameron's face when, by way of a deft and subtle manoeuvre, I sent him hurtling through the air. In my dreams I saw how word of his defeat would spread through the school. He would live out his days in shame and ignominy. I would become the champion of the underdog, like David in his post-Goliath phase.

But July faded into August, and September drew on, and each day's eager scan of the mail produced no jujitsu manual. One day the postman brought me a postcard from the American purveyors of mail order martial arts. It said simply "Item not for sale outside the U.S.A." They did not return my two dollars. I suppose they looked at the unfamiliar Canadian currency and, thinking it was play money, threw it out. I have very mixed feelings about our looming Free Trade arrangements with the United States, but had anyone asked me then what I thought, I would have thrown my lot in with the most rampant of the liberalizers. I went back to school carrying a heavy spiritual burden. Once again, I would be subject to the senseless pummelling of Cameron.

As it turned out he had been moved to another class and had to find a new victim on whom to force his attentions. By some act of grace, no one ever noticed that I was a vacant unit, and I was relatively untroubled for the rest of my elementary school career.

By the time I got into junior high, the emotional wounds had healed over and my battered psyche had been restored. I took my collection of comics down to the book-swap place and traded them in for a battered looking set of the complete works of Dickens.

Now, I recently heard on the news that Archie comics sell more copies in Edmonton than in any other North American city. Perhaps this means the organizers of the Children's Book Festival should target Alberta for an extra-heavy dose of Canadian book boosterism. No doubt the intellectual fibre of those young Edmontonians will be all the hardier if they're encouraged to read the finest of their own country's writing, rather than schlock from south of the border.

I should add however, by way of a tangential postscript, that just the other day I wandered into one of those comic book stores that seem to be springing up all over. There I saw many of the same comics I had read in the early sixties and traded in for Dickens. They were selling for a price that I couldn't begin to think about paying. Had I hung onto my comics for another twenty years I would have been able to retire on the profits and hire a bodyguard who knew everything there was to know about jujitsu. And therein lies a moral that those young Edmontonians would do well to think on.

# LOST CHORDS

Symphony orchestras all across the continent are struggling to keep their heads above water. Flagging attendance, rising costs, dwindling government subsidies: these are the team members that have huddled and come up with killing plays. In Vancouver, after a long period of hearing more of our symphony's maladies than its melodies, the plug was finally yanked. In a way, it was a relief. The childish and public back-stabbing and recrimination-shouting that seemed to be life and breath for the orchestra's board had become a tiresome embarrassment. At least when the orchestra folded and the board members scattered to the wind, we were spared the daily, odouriferous spectacle of so much linen laundering.

The extinction of any orchestra in any city has implications that go beyond the fact of sudden silence. Music education, for example, suffers when musicians move elsewhere. The familial and economic stresses felt by those most closely involved, and by the community at large, are the same as those that arise with any industry shutdown. But as always, the saddest loss is the one that is intangible and can't be quantified. When the Vancouver Symphony went belly-up, we lost a social situation that cannot be duplicated in any other circumstance. For those of us who enjoy the symphony experience this is a great sadness. For those children who may never have the opportunity to hear a live orchestra it is sadder still.

The symphony concert, like a rock concert or a hockey game, has its own code of ethics and conduct, its own time honoured and silly rituals. However vapid these might be, they nevertheless provide a continuum that links one generation of concertgoers to another. I vividly remember the first symphony concert I attended, at the age of ten. The programme was Wagner's *Ride of the Valkyries* (the orchestral version); Schumann's *Piano Concerto in A Minor* (the soloist was Susan Starr, which I thought then and still think is a grand name for a performer); and Brahms's *Second Symphony.*

My grandmother, who had gone to the symphony for years, took me and guided me through it. The whole afternoon unfolded in a prescribed, sure way like a church service. She named the musicians as they drifted onto the stage, took their seats, and noodled through some scales or tricky passages. When they had all assembled, a plump and imperious man carrying a violin strode onto the stage. The audience smacked their palms together. "That's the concertmaster," whispered my grandmother. He pointed a chubby finger at the orchestra and the sweet nasal voice of the oboe sang out. Saw, saw went the strings, and blat, blat went the winds. The concertmaster sat, evidently satisfied by whatever had just occurred, and every eye in the hall focused on the stage right door. It whispered open and the conductor, slim and handsome and slightly dishonest looking, glided to the podium. He was borne along by the affectionate applause of the audience, many of whom, like my grandmother, had done this every second Sunday afternoon for decades. He raised his baton and the great sounds washed across the hall.

I've been to many concerts since in lots of different places. Not all of them have been memorable. But the rituals I witnessed on that first Sunday afternoon, sitting beside my grandmother, have always been dependable. Again and again I have sensed the tension in a hall at the end of the first movement of a concerto, when we all want to applaud but know we musn't and collectively pray that no one will make that gaffe and make the celebrated soloist think that this is a hick town populated by know-nothings. The applause, when it does come, is always a welcome relief, like a hearty sneeze, and the funereally dressed fiddle players always thump their bows to show their appreciation.

A symphony audience is unchanging in its smell: a hundred different colognes and the waft of scotch after an intermission. I have looked forward to developing that peculiar, formal friendship with other season subscribers. I get terrible seats on planes, and almost always find myself with a less than savoury companion. My luck has always been different at orchestra concerts. I have almost always sat beside a peppermint-toting, lavender-sacheted grandmother who leans over and asks, "Well! What did you think of *that*?" And so, not only have I been able to keep the sense of concert ritual alive, I have been reassured by the knowledge that somewhere out there is a whole legion of women who with each passing year take on the duties and responsibilities of generations of grandmothers. "What did you think of *that*?" my own grandmother would ask, every single time. Whenever I go to a concert I am reminded of her, and for me that is no small thing.

All symphony lovers have their own reasons for going from one season to the next. Music is not the least of these. But concertgoing is also about being in a community and honouring the rituals that bind us together as an audience, and bind us to the past. It's a sad thing when those rituals are snuffed out: sad for audiences, sad for the musicians, sad for children who have not yet had the chance to experience the strange, anachronistic, necessary world of the symphony orchestra.

The Vancouver Symphony, luckier than many, was reprieved after many months of soul searching, committee investigations, and breastbeating. Whether it will stick around to enjoy its resurrection or will wing its way skyward, remains to be seen. For a time at least, there will be a place where we can sit together and bask in a wash of sound, perpetuate a piece of the past in the living present, and give it as a gift to the future. And we can find ourselves surrogate grandmothers. And grandchildren. And what do you think of *that*?

## NIGHT-SCHOOL DROPOUTS

*The New Social Peril*

The Gregorian calendar has been with us since 1582. Like most people, I find its "thirty days hath September" arrangement perfectly adequate. In the extremely unlikely event that I should one day be asked to restructure the way we measure time, the only change I'd make would be to shuffle the New Year up to September 1. We all learn from early childhood that this is the real time of new beginnings, new beginnings signalled by the advent of those signs and symbols that mark the start of the school year: fresh hopes, strengthened academic resolve, reinforced sheets of clean looseleaf secured in unscribbled-on binders, and pens with no teethmarks.

This notion is reinforced throughout our lives by the continuing education departments of school boards, colleges, and universities. These agencies, eager to remind us that the brain need not atrophy after final commencement, cram our mailboxes every September with their leaflets and brochures. Who has not agonized over the hard choices with which they present us? Introductory Sanskrit or New Horizons in Origami? Ballroom Dancing or Self-Hypnosis? Automobile Repair or Two Weeks to Better Homemade Yogurt? And once the choice has been made and the requisite number of Tuesday or Thursday nights marked off on the calendar, who has not gone out and bought a few little accessories to refurbish that tired old wardrobe in the hope that perhaps in this class, at last, one will meet that Special Someone? This is September, when hope springs eternal.

What happens, then, during the waning days of October? Why is it that by the time harsh November rolls around, fully fifty percent of night-school registrants have fallen by the wayside? And what becomes of these night-school dropouts? This is a question of pressing concern for welfare agencies the country over. Night-school dropouts are becoming a new menace in our society, one of the hidden but potent ingredients in a simmering stew of social pariahs. You've heard of them. Their sordid stories surface on the back pages of the newspapers. Perhaps you have even seen them loitering around shopping malls, blowing on recorders they've only half-learned to play, trying to sell bad watercolours, being half-assertive with Radio Shack clerks, driving merchants to consider vigilante revenge.

Think what it must be like for these poor souls to come home night after night to a life bereft of purpose, to confront again and again the piercing craft store eyes of a half-finished macramé owl? What pain must be endured by those who have failed to live up to their own vaunted expectations of Szechuan cookery? Every time they go to their kitchen, those shelves of chili oil and pepper sauces offer up their spicy rebuke. What about the severe economic reversals experienced by those who learn, all too late, that their pricey tome on Etruscan ceramics is virtually worthless on the resale market?

Look. I speak from experience. I've been there. I've known the heartbreak. But if you too are a night school dropout, let me assure you that perseverance brings its rewards. Some day you will find a night-school class that will live up to your expectations. It may lie in some unexpected quarter. For me it was musical theatre. I never wanted to take musical theatre. I only registered for it because "Introducing the Didgeridoo" and "Applying the Stanislavsky Technique to Everyday Accounting" were completely filled. As it turned out though, it was a match made in Heaven. I can't explain it. I have a voice that sounds like a garbage compactor, and no dramatic skill whatsoever. It just didn't seem to matter. Week after week I went and inflicted my stunted ability on my much more capable classmates. We had a lovely time. And when the class was done and the time came for our recital, I turned my sentiments about my night-school experience to verse and set them to an old familiar tune. You can sing it for yourself, if you care to.

Try to remember the start of September,
When you were keen and oh-so-eager,
Just what engenders, about mid-November,
The certain sense that you're beleaguered?
By mid-December you'll blush to remember
That long-ago passion for sewing togas;
Take heart, remember, that come next September
    There's yoga.

I wish you could have been there. The applause was deafening.

## YET ANOTHER TURNING POINT

The National Ballet of Canada turned thirty-five in 1987, which means that it has just a few more rings around its trunk than I do. We grew up, the National Ballet and I, almost contemporaneously. Back in the late fifties and early sixties when the ballet was taking its first halting toe-shoed steps towards greatness in Toronto, I was in Winnipeg huffing on the embers of a secret ambition. I wanted to be a dancer. It was an ambition that was not stoked by occasional jaunts to see the Royal Winnipeg. Such excursions would have been right and proper for little girls, but not for the snips and snails and puppy dog tails crowd.

No, my pre-pubescent dream was kept alive by Ed Sullivan. On Sunday nights, after we had consumed the better part of a cow, my parents and brothers and visiting grandmother and I would install ourselves in front of the tube and watch vaudeville die. Sometimes, sandwiched in between the Bulgarian brass band and Tony Bennett, there would be some classical dance. Usually it was a *pas de deux*. Always there would be hoots of derision from my brothers: "What a fruitcake, he's wearing leotards!" And my grandmother would decorously avert her eyes and murmur, "You can see their parts." Too young and too weak-willed to speak my real mind, I toed the party line and snickered along with everyone else. After Ed Sullivan, inspired by the Beatles or Herman's Hermits, my brothers would play air guitar. I would go off somewhere where I wouldn't be seen and practise air ballet. Secrecy was of paramount importance. Back in

1960, if you were a boy and if someone found out that you wanted to be a dancer, you could just kiss your reputation goodbye. Well, to make a long story short, I grew up, and the glowing embers of that desire grew cold and my ambition to dance died and went to vocational heaven. And the world wound on and the National Ballet and I got older, neither sending the other Christmas cards or otherwise keeping in touch.

Then, a few years ago, male dancers suddenly became all the rage. Movies like "White Nights" and "A Chorus Line" brought home the message that dancing is a rigourous and athletic pursuit, that it involves muscles and sweat and nerve and all those other cornerstones of masculinity. This iconization of the male dancer engendered in the hearts of those of us who missed the terpsichorean boat the ludicrous idea that perhaps it wasn't too late. We may never be able to acquire the skill necessary to penetrate the ranks of the corps de ballet, but perhaps we might approximate dancerdom by simply adopting a few simple accessories or mannerisms.

And so I tried. I tried wearing leg warmers. They made my shins itch. Noting that all dancers smoke, I took to the evil weed. Cigarettes nauseated me. I tried to get a dancer's lean and sculpted face. It's impossible to talk when you're sucking in your cheeks. I tried to adopt a dancer's proud and haughty posture. I looked like the "before" picture for a Preparation H ad. I even signed up for one of those dance classes for klutzes. I was asked not to come back.

Finally, I gave it all up. I gave away the leg warmers to an expectant cat who had her kittens on them. I threw away my "If I can't dance, I don't want to be part of your revolution" poster. I resigned myself to the fact that I had passed my prime without ever reaching it. I might have a dancer's soul, but it's welded for the time being to an indigent writer's body. I'm not bitter, though. Tonight I'm going to do some exercises at the bar. And while I'm at it, I'll lift a toast to the National Ballet and wish them another thirty-five years.

# NICE THOUGHTS

Have you ever had that experience of finding that your mind has latched onto a word and won't let it go? The word parades up and down and up and down the shooting gallery of your brain, inviting you to take aim and penetrate its very heart. Take *puddle* for example. Stop for just ten seconds and repeat the word to yourself a few times. Puddle puddle puddle. Isn't it a felicitous combination of syllable, of consonant and vowel? How would the world be different if we called puddle something else or if we used puddle to designate an entirely different concept? "On blustery winter evenings I like to read mysteries beside a blazing puddle."

This kind of speculation, of obsession really, is exactly what you don't need at bedtime. Nothing can be more antisoporific. But it happened to me last night with the word *worry.* Like a spectre out of Dickens, the word rattled its chains and kept me from my sleep. "Worry worry worry," said the voice inside my ear. Sounds like scurry, Surrey, flurry, hurry. I got out of bed and went to the dictionary, hoping to exorcise the ghost. Worry, I learned, comes from the Anglo Saxon *wyrgan,* to choke or strangle. That seemed an appropriate derivation. I took this bit of intelligence and sat down beside the slightly glowing remnants of the puddle and meditated on it. I found myself remembering that as a little boy I was frequently unable to sleep because of worry. I would trudge downstairs and say to my parents, "I can't sleep. I'm worried."

"Oh stuff and nonsense," they replied. "What is there to be worried about? Go to bed and think nice thoughts." And I would try. But imaginings about bunnies and elves just didn't stand up to dark fantasies about the house burning down, or about my father losing his job, or about getting all the way to school before you realized you were bare naked, or about what if I was really adopted?

Sitting there I began to think how true it is that the child is the father of the man, and that I haven't really changed at all since I was a young child. Worry is still the noxious fuel that powers my days. There is just so much to worry about! Why, that day alone I had worried about income tax, the gaping hole in the ozone layer, my deteriorating car upholstery, the Canadian involvement in the slaughter of pigs in Haiti and the consequent disruption of peasant economy. I'd worried about my receding hair line, about some travel arrangments, about whether I'd left the stove on. I'd worried about coffee, about AIDS, about acid rain, about free trade, about cancer, about unemployment, and about everything associated with the word nuclear. Before going to bed I had worried about every single issue raised on "The Journal." I'd even worried about what would happen on the day Barbara Frum wore the same thing twice.

"Think nice thoughts" I heard the old parental voices saying. Well, I reasoned, maybe worry isn't all bad. It's better than complacency. And lots of other people seem to worry as well. Whole industries are built on worry. Face creams for example, to deal with worry-induced wrinkles. Breath fresheners and deodorants to deal with the worry of offending. Bomb shelters, flood control, toilet bowl cleaners . . .

I fell asleep going over that long litany of worry-related products. I woke up around 3 A.M. and went up to bed. I crawled under the covers and closed my eyes. My parents had been right all along. Nice thoughts can win out. I closed my eyes and thought of my parents. My God. What if their retirement funds fail? What if they get sick and have to move in with me? What if I'm adopted?

# STYLE AND SUBSTANCE

There was a time, not so long ago, when candidates for public office were defined as belonging to the Right or to the Left. True, there were all sorts of subspecies that might have evolved in the political woods (such as "somewhat left of centre" or "on the moderate right") but Right and Left were the two poles between which most political discussion navigated. Lately, these two well-worn distinctions have been set aside in favour of Style and Substance.

Every time there's an election each of the two most likely contenders gets saddled with one of those qualifiers.

"He has great style but no grasp of the issues."

"She understands the issues but who wants to listen?"

How often over the course of an election contest does one read or hear this sort of puzzling commentary? Why do people who strive for political recognition never exhibit both tendencies? That style and substance are seemingly mutually exclusive is a sad lesson my own life has taught me. This revelation came to me through the medium of my hair.

My hair has been in eclipse for over a decade. Each day it seems, the glacier of my skull moves slowly but surely along, tearing up the lovely blond turf that once gave it shelter. Each morning I discard on the pillow, in the shower, in the brush, and in a tear-jerking trail behind me, the fruit of my follicles. One day soon, when I speak of my hair, I will no longer be able to use that noun as a collective.

I do not take this lightly. I have done what I can to stem the outward flow. For more than a decade now, I would feel my heart leap at the sighting of yet another shampoo that would promise to restore body, bounce, verve, lustre, and resiliency to my hair, all through the simple trick of balancing my pH.

When finally I stopped believing the extravagant promises of the shampoos, I decided to seek professional assistance. I beat a path to the doors of overpriced stylists in the hope that they would be able to effect some sort of miracle cure. I threw myself on their tender mercies and poured out my deepest fears to them. I solicited their opinions and offered myself up to them as a guinea pig for experimental treatments. I allowed them to fob off on me all manner of costly potions made from rebarbative blendings of desert plant extracts and whale placenta. Willingly I followed the punishing regimens they prescribed. Innocently I forked over 120 smackeroos and received three tiny bottles in which lay the distillation of the hermetic knowledge of some hirsute Finn; three bottles whose contents had to be applied in such a way and at such a time and in such a combination that any social life was rendered impossible.

I watched with growing horror from one year to the next as the prices charged by the hair traffic controllers increased while at the same time their ability to knit my few remaining locks into something resembling a thatch diminished.

And then one day, some months back, I stumbled blindly, pantingly, into yet another salon, hoping against hope that here I would find regeneration. This place had a Japanese name: Tahini, or Sashimi, or something like that. There were all the usual priestesses padding around with their great rainbow manes cascading over their shoulders, muttering their prayers to the musical backdrop of the AM radio. I found myself partnered by a fresh young graduate of the Tahini training programme. Her name was Tracy. She was perhaps eighteen and the bloom of youth on her healthy, chubby cheeks obviated the need for Mr. Revlon's devious assistance. Tracy had only recently come to the big city from her family seat, an orchard somewhere near Penticton. Her country upbringing had instilled in her a sense of no nonsense honesty. I don't doubt that by now her naturally smooth edges have been roughed up by city living. But when I met Tracy she was entirely guileless, and not yet skilled in the devious ways of her professional elders.

"So. What can I for ya?" she asked, picking up my few strands and looking at them as if they were the last tatty remains in a yarn store bargain bin.

"Oh Tracy!" I whined, "Just do something to make it look better than it does. Fuller, you know."

She paused for a long moment. She spun me around in the chair, so that our eyes met directly rather than through the medium of the mirror. She cracked her gum and spoke, her words flying to me on Juicy Fruit scented breath.

"Hey. I can't cut what you ain't got."

To some, this might sound like a harsh indictment. But for me, it proved to be only a tremendous release. All at once, I understood. It was just that old bugaboo of style and substance! I experienced a blinding flash of insight, a satori-like revelation, like Paul on the road to Damascus.

The course of my future life—at least as it relates to my hair—became clear to me. At last, I saw that I must cast off the dreadful yoke which for ten years I had borne. Oh, I knew what I had to do! I leapt from the chair and kissed Tracy sloppily on both cheeks, and shouted out my thanks with the enthusiasm of a miraculously cured leper.

I have now abandoned the chic, chrome-filled halls of the stylists, and I have returned to the sign of the striped pole: the barber shop. It is a transformation that delights me. What formerly cost me twenty-seven dollars now costs me six. No longer do I have my nose rubbed in the seductive promises of stylists' waiting room magazines, like *L'Uomo Vogue* and *l'Esthetica.* Rather, I can leaf through well-thumbed copies of the *Saturday Evening Post* and last year's *Newsweek.* But the most startling change has been in conversation. All the stylists I tried could talk only about new hair colorings, their own hair, or their visits to clubs I had never heard of. Their conversation was windy and brittle and totally without substance. Such is not the case with my barber, Paul. We talk about important things. The weather. The news. Politics.

Style and Substance. You can't have them both. But I've decided I'm a Substance kind of guy myself.

## THE OPEN HOUSE

*A Cautionary Tale*

The time of year has rolled around for us to bid adieu
To dwellings once as quiet as a mouse.
The pressure is upon us all to engineer a do,
The cheerful, festive season open house.

I've asked my friends who each year choose to host these bacchanales
Just why they have them time and time again.
They say, "The season kidnaps us, the merriment forestalls
Remembrance of last year's exquisite pain."

So as a public service, then, I've turned my hand to verse
To try to capture all the agony
Attendant on the Open House. The real thing is worse
Than any poem can ever hope to be.

It doesn't matter at what time your open house begins –
At five or four or even half past noon –
Sure as Joe Clark's got a multiplicity of chins
At least one clown shows up an hour too soon.

Your house is still in chaos and you haven't washed your hair
And neither one can think of what to say,
So you mumble some inanities and bid him have chair
Where he sits and pigs out on your canapes.

Nature's laws are cruel ones – the cat will nab the mouse,
The bear will steal the honey from the hive.
The cosmic rule I find most cruel is at the open house
The dullards are the first ones to arrive.

That first hour you spend clinging to a verbal paddleboard
In the frigid, shallow end of conversation.
You pray, "Dear God deliver me, oh come and take me Lord."
When the doorbell rings and brings you your salvation.

It's jolly Uncle Sidney, his new girlfriend on his arm,
Dear Uncle Sidney, life of every party!
He can crack the ice, he can cajole, kibbitz and charm
With his disarming manner hale and hearty.

Within half an hour the bland atmosphere is charged,
Your guests no longer bill and coo like pigeons.
Dear Sidney ruffled feathers when into the room he barged
With clever jokes about race and religion.

Someone asks you on the sly just who the hell the klutz is,
You try to shrug off Sidney and his stunts.
The doorbell rings a dozen times. Your guests, like tardy buses,
Have all decided to arrive at once.

Marcia brought her baby, Bernie brought his eldest daughter
On Christmas leave from her delinquent school.
She drinks in bars, she hot-wires cars, and last night Bernie caught her
Chasing kittens with his power tools.

And look! There's Jeffrey who last year when he was on a roll
Left you with a present in memoriam:
One last glass of grog and he mistook your goldfish bowl
As something like a Roman vomitorium.

Bob and Mary brought the twins! The minute that you sight them
You rush off to conceal your toiletries.
Last year they inflated several baby stopping items,
And hung them up as baubles on the tree.

Your boss shows up but doesn't stay for more than half an hour,
Your former spouse comes in dressed up in leather,
Her biker boyfriend's attitude is permanently sour,
And he doesn't warm to chat about the weather.

The party doesn't end at five as you had thought it might.
At six more guests continue to arrive.
They show no signs of flagging and in fact after midnight
The open house, unwithered, grows and thrives.

Though nervous fervor kept you going till a while ago
Now, fledgling-like, you want to fly the nest.
The whole thing's gotten out of hand. You've lost that festive glow,
And by this time you don't know half the guests.

You look around and realize that you no longer care.
And muttering nasty words like damn or hell,
You grab a pack of chips and throw some dip in Tupperware
And check in to the nearest cheap motel.

The morning finds you staring at a house that has been through
Some horrifying nuclear event.
You vow that you'll wreak vengeance on the slimy varmint who
Drove a pickup through your picket fence.

And next year when it's time to grease the rusty hosting wheels,
Will you remember how you griped and groused,
And swore that you would keep your door hermetically sealed?
Oh no. You'll say, "Let's have an open house."

## HAMPERS

In the eighth grade I was anointed class president, the only time in my life I have held elected office. I remember the sense of dread that lurched across my stomach when I stepped back into the room from the hallway where I had been banished with the two other contenders while a show of hands was taken. On the blackboard, at the top of a list of three, was my name writ large. According to the custom of the day, the second and third place finishers had been appointed Vice President and Secretary-Treasurer respectively.

I immediately regretted the spasm of vanity that had temporarily robbed me of the sense to graciously decline the nomination. I had never seriously considered the possibility that I might actually attain the lofty office. The other candidates, both boys, were certainly more popular. They were both athletic. Neither wore glasses. Their hair hung over their ears and their collars. They were known to have been out on dates, one of them with a girl from grade nine, which raised his stock considerably. I on the other hand—all myopic, and so socially backward that I didn't even realize it was a serious breach of fashion to carry a briefcase—had nothing whatsoever to recommend me, apart from a kind of devoted bookishness and the fact that I could recite by memory the whole of "The Lady of Shalott," which was no recommendation at all.

How had it happened? I can only conclude that the vote was in some way split, and that I, shuffling in the hallway, was the unwitting spoiler. I might have enjoyed being Vice President, as I have never minded being second best. I could have warmed to the tasks of the Secretary-Treasurer, as there were no minutes to take and no money to tend to, save on the occasional Red Cross Collection Day. But being President carried with it all manner of odious responsibilities, none of which I cared to embrace.

Being President meant you had to attend long and disorganized lunchtime sessions of the student council. These meetings were held in a hot dry room all fusty with the smell of sneakers and antique baloney. There you had to put up with the ravings of nascent radicals who always wanted to dispute the school dress code, or make revolutionary changes to the distribution of weiners on Hot Dog Day. Being President meant you had to scout out pine-panelled rec rooms to commandeer for dreadful parties; parties where bottles would be spun and Ripple Chips slathered in sour cream laced with onion soup mix would be consumed. And being President meant you had to organize the hamper.

This was in Winnipeg, and whether or not the hamper is still a part of junior high school life, I have no idea. But in that dim and distant past the hamper was a project undertaken by all the classes in my relatively well-off and comfortable junior high—ironically named Golden Gate—and its organization fell to the various classroom presidents.

The hamper was a Christmas basket, arranged in co-operation with a social agency, the Christmas Cheer Board. Schools, churches, and service clubs all over the city put them together and delivered them a day or two before Christmas to an assigned family, a family that would otherwise have very little chance of having a happy holiday. My class's family consisted of a mother and her two children, a boy and a girl aged five and eight.

The hamper was the biggest project I had ever undertaken. I was nervous about assuming the responsibility for someone else's happiness, but as time went on I warmed to the task. I drew up lists of items to be included and dictatorially assigned them to my classmates. As the delivery day drew near I nagged those who had not yet brought in their creamed corn, their baked beans, their peas, their Red River Cereal, their Campbell's Cream of Celery soup tins, their big jars of peanut butter, their jams and jellies, their pickles and mustard. I campaigned for toys to be included for the two children. In those sexist days of 1968 dolls were brought in for her, toy trucks for him.

All the while I was nurturing a smug and growing glow of self-satisfaction. In my mind's eye I saw the hearts of the less-fortunate-than-we family leap and gladden upon receipt of this bounty. I saw their startled black eyes grow wide with delight as they opened their unexpected treasures on Christmas morning. I imagined that they would clap their hands and that their sallow cheeks would grow all rosy. Poverty, as the hamper and my imaginings grew, took on a decidedly romantic storybook quality. Although up to that time I had thought I might become a veterinarian, I found myself considering ill-paying but spiritually fulfilling careers as a fulltime engineer of charitable acts, a kind of prairie-bound Father Teresa. That was a long term goal, of course. What was more certain was that at the end of the school year, on Awards Day, my enthusiasm for the hamper would certainly make me a leading contender for our class's Citizenship Pin. It was also likely, given my track record, that I would win the award for academic achievement. The possibility of taking this double crown became the stuff of my dreams. It was the luminous Grail that awaited at the end of the dreadful path of Grade 8.

On the twenty-third of December school dismissed for the holidays and we loaded the three bulging cardboard boxes that were the hamper into my father's car. My own family, at my insistence, had contributed the immense frozen turkey and a Christmas tree. This was strapped to the car roof. My heart was as swollen as the hamper as we drove across the snowy tracks into an unfamiliar part of town, to Stella Street, to make the delivery.

The turf that surrounds the age of thirteen is littered with shattered expectations. The poor were not what I thought they would be. True, our assigned family lived in an apartment building and not a house. But it was reasonably well-maintained. There were no naked bulbs hanging from the ceiling, no plaster lying in the hallways, no overwhelming smell of cabbage. The woman who answered the door was round and pleasant. She did not look defeated or consumptive, not even really tired out. Her children did not come to the door with her, hanging onto her apron strings, their drawn faces a mixture of shyness and eager anticipation. They stayed behind in the living room. I could hear the sound of a television coming from within. A television! They even had a television! She did not burst into grateful tears, did not clutch me to her bosom and say that their lives had been changed forever, did not invite us into her simple home for some weak broth. She simply said, "Thank you. You've been very kind. Merry Christmas." And that was all.

Now, all I really felt as we drove home to Comfort Land was that I had been cheated. After the holidays I would have to stand before my peers and describe the delivery of the hamper. What could I report back to them? Only that it had gone to a family that could have been any one of our neighbours. So what? Big deal! I turned my attention to my own Christmas and the many many things I hoped to get from it.

In the new year I forgot all about the hamper. Certainly it was far from my thoughts when I strode proudly to the front of the gymnasium to receive the Citizenship Pin on Awards Day. The prize for Academic Achievement, however, went to some girl who had crept up on the inside track when I wasn't paying attention. This was the first in what has proved to be a series of very necessary lessons in humility.

The hamper, as it turned out, was also a lesson; one that needed a long time to take root. I have never achieved, nor am I likely to achieve, the kind of easy prosperity that in Grade 8 I had imagined would one day be mine. Nor have I gone in grievous want. But there have been leanish times when it's been all too easy to imagine the possibility of being on the receiving end of charity. On such occasions I think about the hamper and blush to remember who I was. I have nightmare visions of a latter day thirteen year old me coming to my own adult door, staggering under the twin weights of charitable largesse and good intentions.

Heaven forfend! But should such a thing come to pass, I hope that I will have the social skill and good grace of the Stella Street woman and her less-fortunate-than-we family; that I will be able to see through his smarminess to the germinating grown-up inside and, forgiving him and me at the same time, say, "Thank you. You've been very kind. Merry Christmas."

## RUDOLF

*The Real Story*

On Sibir's wild and wind-washed steppes
There lived a happy herd
Of reindeer whose sharp velvet ears
Had never heard a word
That breached their strong communal sense
Of genial detente:
No nightmares born of politics
Rose spectre-like to haunt
The rambling house of dreams where their
Sweet slumber hours were spent.
They woke each morning undisturbed.
Refreshed. Calm. Innocent.

But then one day the gentle wind
Turned sour and blew ill.
(It happened shortly after
Things got hot at Chernobyl)
A reindeer known as Rudolf
(A sound Russian appellation)
Strayed into the path of some
Freewheeling radiation.
He didn't feel a thing of course.
He couldn't guess that ruptures

Were slowly taking place
Within his biorhythmic structures.
He dismissed as sinusitis
A slight tingling in his nose.
Until at dusk a colleague gasped,
And cried: "Good God! It glows!"

The word spread fast, and all the herd
Drew near to gaze upon it,
This prodigal proboscis,
Pulsing, glowing like a comet.
And this was not the only thing
That caused poor Rudolf dread:
That same night phantom voices started
Ringing 'round his head.
He had no way of knowing
That the power plant emissions
Had sensitized his antlers
To freak radio transmissions;
And likewise his compatriots,
Without a point of reference,
Were not inclined to show
Their loony brother special deference.
His glowing nose unnerved them,
The strange mutterings disturbed.
"It's clear," they said, "we'll have to banish
Rudolf from the herd."

The new pariah headed north,
His noise-filled head hung low,
The tundra shining bright beneath
His nose's cheerful glow.
The radio was all he had
To keep him company:
Sometimes Voice of America,
Sometimes the BBC,
Or Radio Moscow filtered through.
One station's diatribe
Against the other made him tremble.

Made him quake and cry.
His heart ached for a place that he
Could find to call his home,
So that he wouldn't have to spend
His life cast out, alone,
With no like mind to comfort him,
To soothe him or console.
And then one day his antlers brought him
"Radio Free North Pole."

"Mayday! Mayday!" came a voice,
All quaking with distress
(Though a quality of jollity
Shone through the SOS.)
Rudolf heard the broadcast through
His gift of wanton fission.
It had to do with an important
Fog-bound mercy mission,
A flying sleigh and reindeer,
And a message of goodwill.
Rudolf's heart lurched throatward,
Then it practically stood still
When the voice asked for a reindeer
Who would hasten north to loan
A sense of navigation
That was flawlessly well-honed,
To lead a team of seven
At a lightning swift sure pace
To pierce the polar mist and make
The world a better place.

Rudolf reared his hoary hoofs
Towards the northern sky;
He scarcely was astonished
When he learned that he could fly.
His antlers were antennae,
And he set a speedy course
And steered himself towards
The urgent broadcast's secret source.

The wee elf who had called him
Was delighted and his team
Of reindeer cried “Three Cheers!
That nose, the brightest ever seen,
Will light the dark; and what is more
As through the sky we shoot
Your antlers will alert us
To the speed traps on our route.”

The elf hitched Rudolf to the sleigh,
The team fell in behind.
They plied the skies to bring their message:
“Goodwill to mankind.”
They took it ’cross the Russian steppes,
And to the fruited plains.
They took it to the palmy south,
And brought it back again,
Back to the Pole where Rudolf lives,
Content throughout the year.
Thus ends this tale. Its name, of course:
Rudolf, the Glasnost Reindeer.

## BRIEF RECOLLECTIONS

I have reached an age when I ought to be able to scan the vast horizon of the years and see looming up from it pinnacles of accomplishment and daring. Alas, all I can survey are a few rounded foothills and the putrid rise that is the landfill site of my experience. I am in my thirties and I have never bought a house, never watched a football game, never played bridge, never contributed to the making of a child. Oh, the list of what I have failed to undertake goes on forever. I won't trouble you with it any further, except to add that I have also never—no, not once—bought underwear. Not for myself. Not for anyone else. This is not because I don't wear it. I do, let me assure you. I would be the last person to go around with my nether bits ungirded, making wanton contact with my clothing.

I have never purchased underwear simply because I have never needed to. When I lived at home my mother bought it for me. She kept a keen eye peeled on the paper for news of any sales. Each Bay Day she'd be elbow to elbow with all the other economy-minded ladies at the underwear bin. I'd come home from school to find my dresser drawer restocked, and the garments I had worn only a day or two before reassigned to a different tour of duty: removing dust from the Toby jugs, for instance.

I have not lived at home in a long time. But I have still never needed to buy underwear. Every year at Christmas my mother sends me a new supply. Usually there are eight pairs: one for each day of the week and a spare to wear on laundry day. I have come to count on this beneficence, just as I count on the certainty of the days' growing longer at the turning of the year.

That my mother will send me underwear just as sure as the sun will rise, is one of the few points of consistency in my life. Jobs, lovers, addresses may change. The underwear is immutable, in both the surety of its arrival and the consistency of its style. The underwear my mother sends – the underwear I am sporting right at this minute – has common sense written all over it. It's a kind of one-size-fits-all brand, born of a mating of cotton and polyester. It's always dark in hue. Navy is the colour my mother favours when it comes to underwear, although she will sometimes sneak in a pair of brown, just to show the versatility of her palette. This is the kind of underwear that used to be featured in newspaper advertisements, the kind that could be safely photographed on stupidly smiling male models without the risk of offending even the most Presbyterian of readers.

Over the years my mother has remained impervious to shifts in underwear fashion. Calvin Klein's naughty ads didn't sway her an inch. It's a good thing, too. If I were to receive a pair of undies that was at all *outré*, I would think that our relationship had taken an unhealthy Oedipal turn. If some Christmas she were to send me skimpy little nylon numbers decorated with hearts or pigs or suggestive slogans like "Home of the Whopper," I don't know what I'd do. I'm just as glad that she sends me the solid, sensible underwear I've always worn.

Like underwear, the human machine eventually wears out. I don't like to think about it, but I know my mother won't be sending me this annual gift forever. Still, if she conforms to the Canadian average, she has more than twenty years of underwear buying left to her. By that time I'll be in my fifties, and I'll probably be hungry for some new experience. I'll think I'll go in for something red. I think I'll go in for something flavoured. And on my mother's birthday, or on state occasions, or on days when my horoscope tells me I'm likely to be run over by a bus, I'll dig out some of those old blue Stanfields. By that time, I should have several trunkfuls.

## CURMUDGEONLY CHRISTMAS

Christmas is a season that's a challenge to curmudgeons,
A time to leave beind our state of bitterest high dudgeon,
A season when we smile upon the klutzes who surround us,
And turn a blind eye to the gross stupidity around us.
I admit I find it difficult to greet with all good cheer
The jerks who cause me misery for fifty weeks a year.
But as a signal of good will, I'll join the festive bleatings,
And send to all life's miseries these happy Yuletide greetings.

To all you grammar guardians who when still in the womb
Squirmed and kicked your mothers when they misused *who* and *whom*,
And who with eagle eye will scan the pages of this tome
With index fingers poised above the buttons of your phone
Primed to dial, to call me up with your familiar claims
That now the good Queen's English tongue will never be the same:
To you I wish a glassy sea, free of linguistic ripples,
And pray a pit bull soundly nips your dangling participles.

And here's my wish for editors, the foul scum of the earth,
The ones who take a manuscript of no uncertain worth
And cover it with coffee rings before they blithely lose it,
And when you call they always say, "Oh that thing, we can't use it."

And who, when they have published something, never once have
failed
To answer payment questions with "Your cheque is in the mail."
Put this festive wish into your Christmas pipe and puff it:
Your magazine's a turkey, buddy, take the thing and stuff it.

And here's to all the drivers at whom I have screamed and roared,
The ones whose cars should bear the warning: Idiot on Board.
The ones who leave my forehead damp with beads of perspiration,
Like those whose left turn signals work on sudden inspiration,
Or those who when they're driving brush their hair and have a chat,
And worst of all – don't ask me why – is men who drive in hats.
To all those drivers who annoy with automotive lapses,
I wish a year of saggy tires, of tickets and speed trapses.

To bank machines that never work, to all rude clerks in stores,
To telephone solicitors and unrepentant bores,
To television preachers and purveyors of junk mail,
To those who talk about their dreams, to friends who never fail
To drop by when you're making love, or when you're having dinner
Just to say, "Oh by the way, your hair is getting thinner."
To everyone involved in the conspiracy to annoy:
Merry Christmas. Happy New Year. Hope that Santa breaks your
toys.

# THE MANY LIVES OF UNCLE GUS

I had another letter from my Uncle Gus in Winnipeg on Monday. Shelley the postwoman didn't look at all like herself. The spring in her step seemed a trifle uncoiled and her usually numinous aura was a mite on the grey side.

"What have you been up to?" I asked. "You look like you've been through the mill and back again."

"Oh, I've had quite a time of it. I spent the whole weekend at a workshop."

Shelley is forever going to workshops of one kind or another. She's deeply involved in New Age disciplines, and given half a chance to talk about it she becomes a kind of evangelist for self-actualization. In the last year she's tried to convince me that my life would be altered for the better if I would only turn over half my income to some aroma therapist, or polarity therapist, or floatation tank emporium. Last month she almost had me convinced to sink a hundred bucks into a three day symposium on coming to grips with nuclear fear.

"But Shelley," I said, "don't you think it's reasonable to feel something like fear when it comes to nuclear weapons? Or nuclear families, as far as that goes."

"No, no. All that stuff is just holding you back! You need to take control. You need to feel personal empowerment." On Monday, when Shelley brought around the letter from Uncle Gus, she looked anything but empowered.

"I spent the whole weekend being rebirthed."

"Rebirthed? My God, Shelley, don't tell me you've been born again!"

"Not in the Oral Roberts sense, no. Rebirthing is a controlled breathing technique that allows the participants to re-experience the trauma of birth."

"You'd probably have a hard time convincing your mother that that was a good idea."

"Oh sure, go ahead and make your little jokes. Flaunt your narrow-mindedness for all the world to see. It just so happens, Mr. Cynical, that the business of being born is every bit as traumatic for the child as it is for the mother. Just think of how awful it must be to be dragged kicking and screaming out of paradise! Much of our adult neurosis can be traced back to that first traumatic experience."

I resisted the urge to say that the most interesting people I know are unhappy and neurotic, and that if they were to disabuse themselves of these qualities they would be but shadows of their former selves. Their stock as dinner guests would fall considerably.

"The rebirthing experience allows you to come to grips with that trauma in a loving and supportive atmosphere. There were six of us who went through it. We screamed for two days solid."

"Sounds swell."

"It was. And now I'm a new woman."

"I suppose you've given up coffee then," I said, running my letter opener through the flap of Uncle Gus's envelope.

She looked past me into the kitchen. She knew she was being tested.

"Got any decaf?"

"No decaf. No light beer. No mild cigarettes. I think that if you're going to have vices you should show them some respect. In fact while you were being rebirthed this weekend, I was out buying an espresso machine."

This was an extravagance that I could scarcely afford, but there are times when you have to make sacrifices to the gods you worship. The new little Cimbali was an attractive altar piece.

"Oh! Oh well then! Maybe a short one wouldn't hurt. In fact, why don't I make it while you see what's up with your Uncle Gus?"

Shelley took over the kitchen and I read her the latest epistle from the prairies.

Weeping Willows Home for Golden Agers
Winnipeg, Manitoba
October 14, 1988

Dear Billy Boy,

As you remember, after your Aunt Adele died I went into the Weeping Willows Home for Golden Agers of my own free will and volition. I'm not one of your old people who think that old breeds old. On the contrary, I liked the idea of playing shuffleboard with a whole lot of grizzled-up codgers. I liked the idea of those organized bus tours to Victoria Beach. I liked the idea of living in a place where people expect you to be cranky half the time, and where they still wait on you hand and foot. I was really looking forward to those high school bands coming to play and to those little kids they always bring in to do highland dancing. In short, Billy Boy, I was looking forward to living in what they used to call an "old folks home."

Well, things aren't what they used to be, let me tell you. A few months ago they hired this woman to come and work here. They call her "The Director of Social Activities." Her name's Briannie. She's a pretty little thing, I must say, and I guess she's plenty smart. She told me she did a degree in sociology, and that her special interest was in Geritol.

"Must mean geriatrics," said Shelley, setting two espressos on the kitchen table.

"Not necessarily," I said, and continued to read.

I'll tell you, Billy Boy, it's been an education having her here. Her head is full of the strangest damned ideas. She just loves to organize these lectures. A couple of weeks ago she had in some woman doctor to explain to us that we could still have satisfying sex lives, even though we're all in our eighties. Heck, we didn't need anyone to tell us that, but I must say that I haven't felt the same about it since I had that trouble with my prostate.

That doctor caused quite a stir though. The same night Helga Havisham came knocking at my door wearing a negligee you could look through and see into tomorrow. I didn't figure she was there to ask for a cup of sugar. "Helga," I said, "it was a lecture, not a set of orders! And besides, 'Gilligan's Island' is on the TV, and I don't want to miss it."

"Oh," said Shelley, sitting down with her espresso. "That's cute!"

I gave her a stern look. I felt offended on behalf of Uncle Gus, who I knew wouldn't look kindly on having his animal instincts dismissed as "cute." I continued to read.

Yesterday, this Briannie told us that there was a hypnotist coming to visit in the afternoon. "That's more like it," I thought. "This'll be a load of fun!" We once had a hypnotist fellow come around to the office Christmas party, way back in '57. Speculation was that the boss, old Sigurdson, had hired him to put Roxy Martin into a trance so that Siggie could get her into the supplies closet. But instead, that hypnotist got Sigurdson up in front of everyone and dangled this big pocket watch in front of his eyes, and before you knew what was happening he had him convinced he was a fish, and he jumped right into the punch bowl. After that, he wasn't good for much. That was one good time, I can tell you.

Anyway, I was really looking forward to the afternoon. About twenty of us turned out for it, and the first thing this hypnotist did was to ask for someone to help him out. I've always been a willing volunteer, so up I went. Billy Boy! It wasn't at all what I figured. It turns out that this fellow had learned hypnosis by taking some kind of course from a correspondence school in California. And he wasn't interested in making people cluck like chickens, or think they were fish. He was all tied up with something called "past life regression."

"Wow!" said Shelley, "That's progressive!"

This fellow believes in reincarnation. He figures that when he hypnotizes someone he can take them back so that they can remember their previous lives. Can you imagine? I can't even remember what I had for breakfast most days. Well, once I found out what he was up to, I wasn't dead keen on continuing. But I figured I might as well give it a shot, seeing as how he'd taken the trouble to come out.

So just you picture this. There I was sitting in this chair in front of everybody, and this fellow says in this real low voice, "I want you to close your eyes. Relax. Tell me how old you are."

"Eighty-four and holding," I said.

"Think back. I want you to remember yourself as you were when you were eighty." I did that. It was easy to remember because that was the year I had that prostate operation. "Remember yourself as you were when you were seventy. When you were sixty."

You get the picture don't you Billy Boy? Back and back we went. Before long, he had me trying to remember what I was like when I was a little boy. Then he said, "Imagine that you're in the womb. It's safe, and warm. Secure. Now," he said, "I'm going to count to ten. And when I say ten, I want you to remember where you were before that moment in time. I want you to look back and see yourself in your previous life."

You know, I felt kind of sorry for this young fellow. I could hear that people were getting a little restless. They'd never seen anything like this before, and it was making them a little uncomfortable. I didn't want to see this guy make a complete ass of himself, so when he got to ten, I started breathing really heavy-like. I groaned a little.

"Do you remember who you are?" he asked me. "What do you see?"

And I did a terrible thing, Billy Boy. I started talking to him in Latin. I gave him the first bit of Caesar's Gallic Wars. We all had to learn it, back when I was in high school.

"Gallia est omnis divisa in partis tres, quarum unam incolunt Belgae, aliam Aquitani, tertiam qui ipsorum lingua Celtae, nostra Galli appellantur. Hi omnes lingua, institutis, legibus inter se differeunt. Gallos ab Aquitanis Garumna flumen, a Belgis Matrona et Sequana dividit." That was about all I could recall, so I just did a bit more panting, and muttered "Quo vadis," and "Quid pro quo" under my breath for a bit, and conjugated a few verbs. Then I pretended to snap out of it.

I felt badly pulling his leg like that, but it sure was a good joke. I figured that he wouldn't have much of a classical education, and I was right. When I opened my eyes and saw him looking at me like he'd seen a ghost.

"That was remarkable,' he said. "I've heard of subjects speaking in strange languages before, but I've never seen it myself. I can't be sure, but it sounded to me as though it might have been Latin."

"You don't say."

"Amazing. I wonder if you could have been a Roman senator. Perhaps you were even Caesar!"

"Wouldn't that be something!" I said.

So I sent him away happy. And that night, Helga Havisham came and knocked on my door again. "Helga!" I said, "What the dickens are you wearing? I can see the scar from your appendectomy." "Oh Gus," she said, "I've had the most remarkable vision! I saw so clearly that in an earlier life I was Cleopatra! Whatever do you make of that?"

So I asked her to come in. These might be my salad days after all, Billy Boy. They just might be. Regards to Shelley.

Affectionately,
Uncle Gus.

"*Et tu*, Gus," said Shelley. She took the espresso cups to the sink and put on her Walkman. She cranked up the volume and walked off listening to her New Age music and looking much more herself.

## CROSSING THE BOARDER

*". . . the heart of me weeps to belong*
*To the old Sunday evenings at home . . ."*
D.H. Lawrence, "Piano"

Last Sunday night as I sat down
To bland fast-frozen victuals
I recollected childhood days,
And their elaborate rituals.

Our Sunday meals of long ago
All featured beefy treats
That Dad would carve while Mom decried
The high price of red meat.

And every Sunday evening
When the roast had bit the dust
We'd climb in dad's De Soto
And we'd visit Uncle Gus.

We'd drive across the city
To his house in St. Vital
Where he lived with his six hamsters
And with sainted Aunt Adele.

My dad would bring a bottle,
And my mom would snip sweet peas
These latter were for Aunt Adele.
We'd find her on her knees

Purging dandelions from
Her clipped, well-tended lawn.
She'd wave to us when we drove up,
While Uncle Gus would yawn

And rise from his post-prandial nap
Upon the porch. "How nice
To see you folks! You've brought some rye!
I'd better find some ice.

"I think I've got some Seven too.
I'll go and snap some lids,
And if you old folks say I can,
I'll pour some for the kids."

"Well, I don't know," my dad would say
"I'm not sure that you should."
Then we would whine and clamour
That we'd each of us been good.

(Oh how naive that we believed
That virtue carried leverage!)
Old Gus would chuckle and pour out
Our carbonated beverage.

We'd gulp it in an instant
And then vainly try to squelch
The fizzy consequences:
Mom would grimace when we'd belch.

Aunt Adele would fetch a vase
And fill it at the sink,
"Sweet peas! They're my favourites!"
"Would you take a tiny drink?"

Uncle Gus would ask her.
She would smooth her Sunday skirt
And blush a little when she said
"A wee one wouldn't hurt."

We'd sit down in the parlour
And dissect the week just gone,
With a break from conversation
When Ed Sullivan came on.

Once Henny Youngman had his say,
And Steve and Edie'd sung
We'd talk about the plans we'd made
To fill the week to come.

Then Uncle Gus rose from his chair
And said "Who'd like some more?"
We'd squirm a bit and ask if we
Might go out to explore.

(For with the second glass of rye
The adults got all vexed
And started singing sordid songs
Of politics and sex.)

"You kids behave," my Mom would say.
"Aw, heck," Gus said, "they're fine.
Just keep clear of the marigolds,
Don't bother Mr. Stein."

A shiver overtook us then,
It gripped our very guts.
We'd step outside and fantasize
Soon as the door was shut

About the dire and dreadful things
That we'd be sure to find
Within the locked and grisly lair
Of evil Mr. Stein.

See, Gus had fixed his basement up,
He'd made a furnished suite.
He ran an ad soliciting
A tenant who was neat

And quiet and responsible,
And Mr. Stein applied.
He'd lived there for a dozen years
But never been outside:

At least not on a Sunday night
When we had come to call.
We'd never seen him once, and yet
He held us in his thrall.

For every single Sunday
Gus's voice came through the rye:
"You musn't cross the boarder!"
But he never told us why.

He never said why Mr. Stein
Should never be disturbed
Nor why our boyish tendencies
To ruckus should be curbed.

The mystery of Mr. Stein
Commanded our attention.
And since we had no concrete facts
We gave way to invention.

"Whattaya think he looks like?
Is he fat or is he thin?"
Around the basement window
We'd try vainly to peer in,

And speculate at what we'd see
If we could look behind
The never-opened barrier
Of his Venetian blinds.

His corporal incarnations
Varied widely as time passed.
Sometimes he was a hunchback
With his face scarred by the blast

That rocked his laboratory on
The night he tried to make
A monster who would rule the world!
Three pairs of knees would quake

At stories we would fabricate
Of simple-minded fools,
Demented dwarves, or babbling goons
With faces streaked by drool.

"I bet that he's a Nazi,"
Said my older brother Bert,
As with a twig he sketched a crude
Swastika in the dirt.

"I bet he has a freezer full
Of murdered dogs and cats,"
Ventured Jim, my little brother,
"And I'll even bet you that

"If he heard us talking 'bout him
He would put us in there too."
"I guess," I said, "but first I know
Exactly what he'd do.

"He'd lock us all in cages,
And he'd throw away the keys,
And he'd feed us slugs and mothballs
And he'd never set us free,

He'd cut our toes and noses off
And bake them in a pie."
"Stop!" cried Jimmy, who commenced
To bellow and to cry.

"Goddam kids," my father'd mutter
As he came out of the door.
"What's going on?" my mother'd say,
"I've told you three before

To smarten up. Why can't you learn?
This happens every time!
Jimmy! Hush! You'll wake the dead!
You'll wake up Mr. Stein!"

Then Jim would cough and splutter
And again the tears would flow.
Our parents heaved a heavy sigh.
"I guess we ought to go,"

They'd say, and patient Aunt Adele
Would make a clucking noise.
"Don't you worry, they'll be fine,
They're boys who will be boys."

"Come back again," said Uncle Gus,
"Goodbye, goodbye!" we'd wave.
And they'd wave back, but nothing moved
In Mr. Stein's dark cave.

The old De Soto headed home,
Goodbye to St. Vital,
Goodbye to yet another night
With Gus and Aunt Adele.

Dad would tune the radio,
And sometimes he would find
A funky Motown station
That had snuck across the line

From far off Minneapolis.
"Damn racket," he'd complain
And turn the dial until he found
Glen Yarborough again.

While driving home we'd argue
Over whether that faint star
Was actually a planet:
Venus, Jupiter, or Mars.

We'd count each passing Volkswagen:
We might have counted sheep,
For by the time that we got home
We three were fast asleep,

Dreaming of the day when we
Would grow up and could order
Children to be quiet,
And to never cross the boarder.

The year that Aunt Adele gave in
To cancer's hard-sell line,
Gus sold the house and bade goodbye
To evil Mr. Stein.

It seems to me I heard that he
Went to his sister Laura
Who had a house in Thunder Bay,
Or possibly Kenora.

It doesn't really matter:
Childhood's gone and Sunday's lost,
And Stein will stay a boarder
That we never dared to cross.